Why Bother? Why Not!

Why Bother? Why Not!

A Hollywood Insider Shows You How to Live Like a Star, in a Snap!

Laurin Sydney

Coanchor of CNN's
Showbiz Today

Cliff Street Books

An Imprint of HarperCollins*Publishers*

HarperCollins books may be purchased for educational, business, or sales promotional use. For information please write: Special Markets Department, HarperCollins Publishers Inc., 10 East 53rd Street, New York, NY 10022.

First Edition

Designed by Joel Avirom and Jason Snyder
Design assistant: Meghan Day Healey

Photographs copyright © 2000 by Rick Szczechowski and Tom Eckerle

Watercolors copyright © 2000 by Marian Nixon

Printed on acid-free paper

Library of Congress Cataloging-in-Publication Data

Sydney, Laurin, 1954-
Why bother? Why not!: a Hollywood insider shows you how to live like a star, in a snap! / by Laurin Sydney.
p.   cm.
ISBN 0-06-019586-X
1. Entertaining. I. Title.
GV 1472.S93 2000
793.2—dc21   00—030338

00 01 02 03 04 ❖/RRD 10 9 8 7 6 5 4 3 2 1

To the laughing, loving spirit of

My Tess and Sid

XOXOXO

Acknowledgments Each year,

during the telecast of the Academy Awards, I am definitely one of the few who think the acceptance speeches should be longer! How can you possibly give a heartfelt thanks in 1½ minutes? Now, I face the same dilemma in acknowledging my heartfelt appreciation to all of my book angels in just 1½ pages . . . But the show must go on!

A standing ovation to my supersensational editor, friend, and founder of Cliff Street Books—the brilliant Diane Reverand, who at the very beginning promised that we would have fun! To the wonderfully supportive and gentle Janet Dery and the rest of the Harper-Collins clan, the talented eyes of Joseph Montebello, Richard Rhorer, Pam Pfeifer, Margaret Meacham, Shelby Meizlick, Keeva Mosher, and Doug Didyoung.

A thousand bows to one of the best people on the planet: my incomparable agent and incomparable friend, who makes everything she touches "Jan Millerish." And to the rest of the hard-working gang at Dupree Miller in Dallas.

Thunderous applause to designer extraordinaire, Joel Avirom, who along with Jason Snyder and Meghan Day Healey, did backflips to make everybody happy. To the talented and patient Marian Nixon—who can illustrate my life anytime.

Rousing cheers to the genius, love, and friendship of my longtime makeup artist, Amy Macar, and to two picture perfect people and photographers, Rick Szczechowski and Tom Eckerle. To Richie Arpino, who kept our spirits and my hair bouncy during the photo shoot.

An encore of thank-yous to all of the following fabulous folks who contributed their spirits to the cause—Über friends, Norma and Marvin Lesser, for always being my loving anchors . . . Matt Carey, Susan Estrich, Christina Sidoti, and Steven Einhorn, Muffin Gifford, Lynne Lester, Perri Peltz, Sarah and Steve Kramer, Rolf Sjogren, Jose Eber, Al Rubin, Nadia, Madison, Max, Sydney, and Dellwood Huberman . . . Mike Gittelman, Al DiSanti, Charles Hawkins, Karen Curry, Anita Plotkin, Michael Huberman, Cass Carmel, David Evangelista, Katie Koras, Phyllis Kohut, Barb Griffen, Kerri Murphy, Shari Mesulam, Rick Kaplan, Rene and Kopel Burk and Daniel Weber. My brilliant designer, Pilar Rossi and hair color genius, Johanna Stella, Jen Zaldivar, Tom Allee, Howard Polskin, Karen Bonsignore, John Valdestri . . . My angel, Nicole Van Ruden, Jill Brooke, who first said "Why don't you write a book?" and of course I am always grateful to Kristina Martin.

Raise that curtain for my loving gang at CNN Showbiz, New York . . . starting with the Big Kahuna Boss Guy, Scott Leon, who helped in every way imaginable to facilitate this book. And to the rest of my work family, including Marc Balinsky, Lori Blackman, Jennifer Goldberg, Adam Kluger, Jamie Mendelovici, Laura Molta, Michael Okwu, Mark Scheerer, Cynthia Tornquist, Bill Tush and Rachel Wells. Your daily support through all of my facacta projects is soooo appreciated . . .

I give the star treatment to Jane and Michael Huffington, whose "mi casa es su casa" attitude is incredible and priceless. To my priceless brother Tiger—whose spirit is applauded by everyone he knows.

Rip open the award envelope for Yvette Fromer for being the winner that I've always known she is.

A round of applause for some inspirational Why Bother, Why Notters—Margret Pond, Sandee Moss, Lori Kennedy, Lisa Aikee Raphael

Acknowledgments

Sparge, and Anne Lenox, Kristina Martin, Normi Lesser, Rosemary D'Amato, Steve Salinaro, Jane Hoffman, and Lynn Huberman.

🔍 Shower her with Sweetheart Roses . . . Dana Horn, who has been the backbone of this book, from the first syllable to the end. Her heart, commitment, brainpower, enthusiasm, and fingers are unequaled in my world!

🔍 And the Oscar goes to Lynn Huberman, and not because of nepotism (She happens to be my beautiful, loving sister)—she also happens to make magic when it comes to prop and food styling. Match that with her tireless, egoless perfectionism, and how lucky am I! She's a miracle worker!

🔍 And as the curtain goes down on these acknowledgments (I know it's corny, but it works), I need to stop the show for my fella . . . who gave up countless nights and weekends of "us" time for "book" time. . . His never-ending, unselfish support of my needs is astonishing, and gives me one more reason to adore him! Thank you, Planey! My love, thanks, and kudos to all.

*Introduction

Why Bother? Why Not! Especially since it doesn't require a lot of **Time**, **Talent** or **Money** . . . to make your lifestyle and the lives of people around you more satisfying and special. And guess what? It doesn't even require a glue gun. I don't even know where a hardware store is. You already have the main tool you'll need, but most of us never "bother" to use it. It's called creativity.

As the cohost of *Showbiz Today*, CNN's worldwide entertainment news program, I've been peeking into the lives of superstars for the past 10 years. I've hung out with **Tom Cruise** and his disgustingly beautiful wife, **Nicole Kidman**, in a cabana on the Mediterranean . . . got all steamy steaming clams with **Mel Gibson** in Maine . . . strummed with **Springsteen** . . . gabbed with **Garth** . . . dined with royalty . . . picnicked on the beach in the south of France with **Jim Carrey** . . . attended one of **Elizabeth Taylor**'s eight weddings . . . debated politics with **Robin Williams** . . . and cooked alongside Spago's **Wolfgang Puck**, as he prepared dinner for 3,196 starving celebrities at the Academy Awards Governor's Ball.

I'm not telling you this to brag about my frequent-flier miles, I simply want to share what I've learned (especially since you've already bought this book!). After a decade of observing the charmed lives of some of the most celebrated people of our time, I've found that many of the "touches" that go into their magical lifestyles are not beyond the

reach of all of us. It's not about an unlimited pot of gold—it's about an attitude.

I've always been a gal who *"bothered"* around the home, around the workplace, and in my relationships—putting that extra little effort into almost everything I do. How do I have the time? Well, just like you, I don't, nor do I have an abundance of talent or spare cash. But that's not what it takes.

When a flu-laden **Steven Spielberg** came to an interview with a 102° fever, I appreciated his effort. He knew that he could not reschedule and the show had to go on. Later in the day, I sent him chicken soup from the Carnegie Deli in New York in a brown paper bag. I received such a doting thank-you note, you would have thought I gave him the foreign-distribution rights to *E.T.* This is a man who could afford to have every deli chef in the world on his payroll, but he appreciated the fact that I *"bothered."* Because while it's always easy to say **"why bother?"** I always say **"why not!"**

For instance, if **Brad Pitt** was on location in Dayton, Ohio, and was coming to your house for dinner (don't ask questions, just play along) would you bring the Kraft Singles in their individual wrappers to the table? What about the Heinz bottle with the old crusted layers of ketchup around the neck? And would you use that pile of old news-papers, bills, and clean socks as the centerpiece on your table?

No. You would at least wash the top of the ketchup bottle and put the socks back in the drawer. But then what?

This "how to" book will prepare you for that dinner with Brad Pitt—but just in case he doesn't come a-calling, this manual will teach you how to put that extra little effort into everything you do. It won't provide you with unlimited green stuff and an entourage, but it just might make you and those around you feel like a star.

For many years, a lot of my waking hours have been spent answering SOS phone calls such as,

"How do I gift wrap a new car?"

"Help! I have forty-five minutes to throw together an elegant dinner for my husband's ex-wife!"

"How can I possibly thank my veterinarian for saving my dog's life?"

"I have to impress my boss, whom I detest. What can I buy?"

"I have to plan a third-birthday party for twins. What can I do that's different?"

The questions go on and on and so do the answers, with creativity at the core. Please have fun with this book; keep it handy and use it as a springboard for your own ideas. Soon it will become a "way of life," and you'll be writing your own chapters.

This is a lifestyle book about styling your way of life. Along the way I'll share some celebrity tricks of the trade that you can incorporate into your daily living. I realize that not every task requires the same effort, so I've divided the solutions into **"Baby Bothers"** and **"Big Bothers."** You decide how far you want to go.

And the next time you exert a little extra effort and your mother-in-law (who has bought you the same scarves with the little Scottie dogs on them for the past eight Christmases) says to you, **"why bother?"** a smile and a simple **"why not!"** will say it all.

Your Presents Are Required

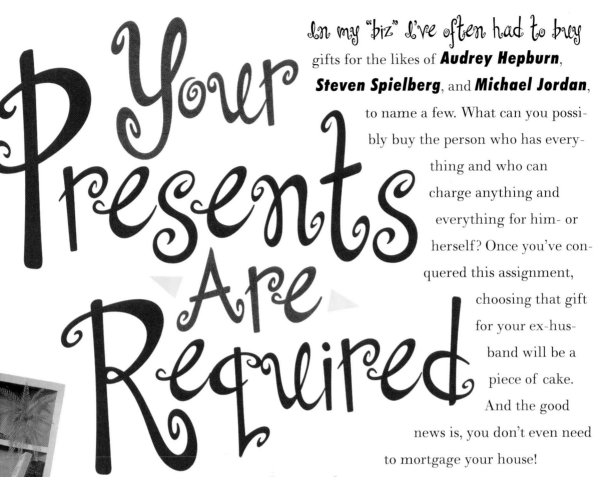

In my "biz" I've often had to buy gifts for the likes of **Audrey Hepburn**, **Steven Spielberg**, and **Michael Jordan**, to name a few. What can you possibly buy the person who has everything and who can charge anything and everything for him- or herself? Once you've conquered this assignment, choosing that gift for your ex-husband will be a piece of cake. And the good news is, you don't even need to mortgage your house!

When I had to buy **Audrey Hepburn** a thank-you gift for a favor she had done for me, I packed a Tiffany bag with one dozen of her favorite New York bagels (poppy seed, by the way). They were from H&H bagels (2239 Broadway, New York, NY; 212-595-8003), who will FedEx their bagels to wherever you live. It was *Breakfast at Tiffany's* for $4.95 and she loved every bite.

I interviewed super hoopster **Michael Jordan** about his men's perfume line and agreed that the scent was like sex in a bottle. I later emptied a bottle of the aphrodisiac and filled it with a subscription to a provocative magazine—a tailor-made present, all in good fun. It was a slam dunk.

TIFFANY & CO.

And speaking of "Taylor-made" presents, when **Elizabeth Taylor** jetted to the south of France to host her annual AmFAR event, an Hermès leather bag filled with lilac roses awaited her in her villa (this was obviously not courtesy of 1-800-FLOWERS).

When you're having trouble finding just the right little somethin', don't, I repeat **don't**, go shopping. First sit down and think creatively. In the realm of gift giving, ingenuity is priceless.

And for Pete's sake, if you're not going to listen to me and you're on your way to the store to buy a tie for your boss, at least drop a tie around a wine bottle with a note that says, "Tie one on for your birthday." You may not get a raise, but you will get an honorable mention!

And if you'd rather **Buy Than Try . . .** don't worry—I have many fantastic foolproof gifts up my sleeve that are merely a credit card away.

In this chapter, you'll also find the formula for selecting just the right little somethin' for a birthday, wedding, anniversary, get-well wish, and any of the other marvelous miscellaneous occasions that come up in your life.

Birthdays, Weddings & Anniversaries

I am not suggesting that you get married on your birthday, but since the thought processes behind these three categories are so similar, I've combined them to save you reading time.

Baby BOTHER

Okay . . . where do you start? How do you begin to develop your gift-giving technique? Well, it's easy to begin with numbers when you're dealing with birthdays or anniversaries. Have the celebrated number correspond with the amount of items. For instance . . .

- 🔍 *23* **lottery tickets** for a 23rd birthday
- 🔍 *23* **golf balls** for a 23rd birthday (provided your friend plays golf)
- 🔍 *23* issues of a favorite **magazine**
- 🔍 *23* prepaid gallons of **gas**
- 🔍 *23* **movie tickets**
- 🔍 *23* **cigars** (when applicable)
- 🔍 *23* **Twinkies** (can go a long way for the right person)
- 🔍 *23* **donations** to his or her favorite charity

If you're having trouble coming up with items, think about your person's personal passion.

Big BOTHER

Now, if you have your thinking cap on, take it off, cuz it will really mess up your hair. But get ready to think of **23 different** presents for a 23rd anniversary. . . . Yes, you do need to bother a bit, but boy is it worth it! These gifts should be very personal. It's hard for me to lead you down the "yellow brick road," not knowing your cast of characters, but these generic ideas might help.

Music Memories

It's very easy to go on the Net and find out the #1 song of a particular year. Armed with that knowledge, Bleeker Bob's Golden Oldies in New York's Greenwich Village (212-475-9677) can most likely locate any album, CD, or 45 ever recorded. Your local music store can also order hard-to-find CDs at no extra charge. You can also e-mail your requests to BB@aol.com.

Better With Age

Your local liquor store may stock old bottles of wine, including one whose year corresponds with the date you're looking for, whether it's the year in which your couple was married or your "celebrant" was born. If you can't find your bottle locally, try Sherry-Lehman Wine Shop in New York City (212-838-7500).

Calendar Girl (or Boy)

Kinko's puts together a great personal calendar using your photos for $36.95. Your pictures are laminated and positioned as monthly cover pages in an 8 x 10 spiral calendar. The pix can correlate to occasions in the month, and the year can begin whenever you choose. If the birthday is in October, the calendar can go from October to October.

Remember, not all of these assorted presents need to cost money. When I procured 45 different presents for my in-laws' 45th anniversary, I included:

- A $3.75 **cookie** from Dean & DeLuca in SoHo (212-226-6800) that was in the shape of a pug—their first dog together

- **Matches** from the restaurant where they first met

- A **postcard** from the town where they first lived

- A **wine bottle** from Scribble It, an adorable store in Newton Highlands, Massachusetts (617-964-9897), that imprinted their names along with "Vintage 45 years." They will customize wine bottles filled with candy, nuts, etc. The label can say anything you want, such as "Lucy and Ricky: Like fine wine Est. 1952" or "Grandma Becky: Sweet as sugar at 83." This bottle will set you back only $19.95.

- A computer **mouse pad** with their honeymoon picture superimposed on it

- **Sheet music** of the song that they danced to at their wedding

- 45 **custom pencils** from the Lillian Vernon catalog that said, "Still Getting the Point After 45 Years" ($9.95 and they'll print whatever you want!)

- Scribble It also makes a personalized **ceramic house**, signifying when the couple was "established" in their first home . . . and your down payment is only $35!

Keep in mind that the more personal you get with these multiple gift ideas, the better. And don't forget to share the responsibility with other members of your family. Delegate. You don't have to do it all! Now, on to other creations.

Baby BOTHERS Present of the Month Club

And you're the president! To celebrate a wedding, birthday, or anniversary, why not spread the cheer throughout the year. Everyone can benefit from a monthly boost. So why not start a "Present of the Month Club"? Each month, send or hand-deliver your trinkets to the lucky recipient. You can choose to send these treats for a whole year or less. Of course, there are companies that do this with items such as beer and flowers, but if you do it yourself, you can customize the gifts and save yourself some money. Think about sending different versions of the following. . . .

- **Underwear** (male or female)
- **Designer waters**
- **Chocolates**
- **Designer sodas**
- **Diet salad dressings** (don't laugh, these will go over like gangbusters with the right person!)
- **Cigars**
- **Melons**
- **Champagne** (you can do little splits to save money)
- **Herbs** (dried or fresh)
- **Baseball caps**
- **Fancy soaps**
- **Shampoos and conditioners**
- **Olive oils**

- **Movie tickets**
- **Best-sellers**
- **Lipsticks**
- **Teas or coffees**
- **Golf balls**
- **Videos**
- **CDs**
- **Stationery**

The list is endless . . . and so is the pleasure to the person who receives a gift a month!

Wedding Bell Blues

This idea also works well for anniversaries as well as weddings. We're gonna go back to basics by simply buying or finding something old, something new, something borrowed, something blue. Some people have trouble finding the something blue. I've given Skyy Vodka, which comes in a blue bottle . . . Blue Water cologne by Davidoff . . . Blue Point Oysters . . . a blue bonnet bouquet . . . even a Blues Brothers CD!

Basket Case

Traditionally, the celebrity presenters of the Academy Awards don't get to take home any gold statuettes . . . but they do get to take home a generous basket of souvenirs on Oscar night. Some of the loot given after a recent ceremony included:

🔍 A Baccarat crystal pendant

🔍 A Harry Winston sterling silver compass

🔍 A JBL stereo CD system

🔍 A Mont Blanc Wolfgang Amadeus Mozart pen

🔍 A Tag Heuer watch

🔍 A Steiff teddy bear

🔍 A bottle of Mumm Cordon Rouge Champagne

On the small screen, the **Emmy Award** gift basket contained around 4,000 bucks worth of goodies . . . featuring a week's consultation with a celebrity nutritionist (liposuction not included). But it was the **VH1 Diva Awards** gift basket that took the cake. It included custom "diva" cookies from *Eleni's* in New York City (212-255-7990). If you can dream it, they can bake and ship it.

Even though your pockets may not be as deep as the Academy's, you can still create perfect, personalized baskets faster than you can see a nominated movie. You can do these baskets for multiple occasions.

Expand your thinking by focusing on people's passions. We all know the usual stuff in gift baskets, so try to push beyond that. Some unusual ideas include:

A French Toast Basket Include Grandma's recipe, pure genuine maple syrup, country eggs, great Tuscan bread, cinnamon sugar, vanilla beans, and a beautiful ceramic mixing bowl.

A Lemon Basket Of course, throw in a couple of lemons . . . then add lemon shampoo, a lemon zest tool, lemon-scented shelf paper, and lemon-ade mix (if you include some lemon drops and lemon cookies it becomes a sweet-and-sour basket).

A Beach Basket A waterproof radio, a blow-up plastic pillow, sunburn relief spray, and nonfat cookies (since bathing-suit season is 30 seconds away).

A Couch Potato Basket Two Idahos for baking, a *TV Guide*, microwave popcorn, a neck-support pillow, and a blank VHS tape.

A Pearly Whites Basket A brand-new high-tech toothbrush, European toothpaste, a rinse cup, flavored floss, and mouthwash transferred to a pretty jar (your dentist will love you!).

A "Don't Pull Your Hair Out!" Basket A ponytail scrunchie, luxurious aromatherapy conditioner, a brand-new brush and comb, shine pomade, European color-enhancing shampoo, and a hair-styling magazine.

A Pedicure Basket Polish, cotton balls, remover, file, moisturizing foot cream, and an adorable pair of rubber flip-flops to make drying more fun.

Alphabet Soup If you can't thread a needle, I bet your local tailor can. I would also bet that he or she has a little gizmo that attaches to his or her sewing machine to make monogramming an inexpensive breeze. But why stop with initials. Let yourself go—think names. Think phrases. Turn a simple towel into a great gift.

On golf towels:

- *Bob's Bogey*
- *Peter's Putter*
- *Uncle John's Under*
- *No Traps for Tom*
- *My Handicap's 11 and Rising!*

On tennis towels:

- *Love Linda*
- *Steve's Serve*
- *Zelda Navratilova*
- *Morris McEnroe (you're allowed!)*

On dish towels, call attention to someone's specialties or lack thereof:

- *Mabel's Matzo Balls*
- *Kathy's Key Lime*
- *Chef Suzie*
- *David Always Dries!*

On handkerchiefs, send a get-well or supportive message, or simply stitch a name.

On socks . . . Why advertise Nike? How about adding some identification? Little grown-up ones love it.

- *Scott's Right*
- *Scott's Left*

Remember, practically anything can be monogrammed, including stuffed animals, dolls' clothes, and lunch box napkins. These gifts are thoughtful, inexpensive, and one of a kind.

Charity Begins at Home
A Hollywood giving trend that has become fashionable over the past few years is notification that "a charitable donation has been made in your name." Naturally, since you are the one doing the donating, you should pick causes that are close to your heart. But do your homework to find out which charities are important to your recipient as well.

One darling of the Hollywood set is the *Elizabeth Glaser Pediatric AIDS Foundation.* Some of the foundation's star-studded supporters are **Jack Nicholson**, **Robin Williams**, and **Tyra Banks**. Another celebrity diligently devoted to improving the lives of children is **Rosie O'Donnell**. Her charity, *The For All Kids Foundation*, has awarded more than 300 grants to nonprofit organizations that help children.

The idea that small acts of kindness can produce unbelievable results inspired **Oprah Winfrey** to launch *Oprah's Angel Network,* a charity devoted to helping people in need.

Horse Sense
It's a good thing I have my own teeth, because if I had false ones, they would have fallen out one beautiful evening in Malibu, California. The sun was setting over the Pacific at a clambake given by a huge Hollywood honcho. I thought I was quite clever when I presented my host with four antique, handmade lobster bibs. He gave me a quick thank-you and went back to convulsing over the gift that someone else had just given him . . . a racehorse . . . yup . . . a racehorse.

The wonderful **Michael Landon**, who was standing next to me, whispered, "I wish he'd given that money to charity." And from that moment on, I have added donations to my host's favorite charity to my "one night only" repertoire. Sorry, Mr. Ed.

✶ For the Bride and Groom Only ✶

Whoever invented the idea for the bridal registry should be given the Nobel Peace Prize. Who has time to return 37 pairs of candlesticks or Uncle Harry's ugly ice bowl? But if you want to impose your gift-giving creativity on the happy couple, that's fine by me. Let's create.

Be Part of the Honeymoon

No, don't pack your bags . . . this is a spiritual journey. With the couple's itinerary in hand, decide how you would like to participate.

1 Have flowers, wine, or champagne delivered to one or more of their destinations during their trip.

2 Prepay a private tour guide.

3 If the hotel will accommodate you, hire a masseuse for an in-room massage.

4 Award a photo scholarship: tell the couple that you would like to take care of all their honeymoon photo costs (include an interesting album if your wallet allows).

Culture Shock

The honeymoon is over and now what? Get your couple a membership to a local museum or one in a nearby city. As a bonus, you can include a gift certificate for the museum gift shop. If art is not on their radar screen, get them a subscription to their local theater group. Okay, okay . . . if these ideas are too highbrow, how about a pair of seats to an upcoming rock concert (presented in the group's CD), or, as long as they're both into it, a sports event (given in a baseball cap)?

Training Wheels

All brides and grooms put on a couple of pounds right after their wedding, because they don't have to squeeze into that dress or tux anymore. As a wedding gift, give your couple some sessions with a private trainer. Their thighs will thank you.

A~dress

No, I'm not asking you to contribute to the wedding gown, I'm talkin' about the street where they live. Even though we now live in an e-mail environment, beautiful stationery is always welcome. Have it engraved with the new Mr. & Mrs. name and address.

The Clean Machine

And we're not talking vacuums here. Bestow upon your couple a spring-cleaning service who will come into their apartment or home and scrub-a-dub-dub. I know it's not romantic, but it will leave more time for romance.

Second Honeymoon

After all the rice has been thrown and your couple has returned from cloud nine, provide them with an oasis in town that they can use on a special night. Prepay for a room or suite at a local hotel (including breakfast in bed) and, before they arrive, arrange for a framed wedding picture to be placed on the nightstand in their room.

Stretch

Hire a limo for the night so the newlyweds can whoop it up at their disposal. Make sure it is a reputable company since you will need to prepay.

Newlyweds **Courteney Cox** and **David Arquette** have good "friends" like **Brad Pitt**. At their wedding, they showed their appreciation to their buddies by giving each guest a beautiful gift box filled to the max with a bonanza of bath items and romantic candles. A lovely idea from the bride and groom . . .

Get-Well Goodies

Whether your patient has the sniffles or a serious illness, the best get-well presents enhance life. Whether you're tickling a funny bone or soothing a broken bone, please make sure your gifts are health appropriate.

The Band-Aid Played On

If someone is ill and you want to act quickly, an e-mail or phone call may not be what the doctor ordered. Just go to your medicine cabinet, pull out a trusty Band-Aid, include it in a little note, and you have an instant get-well wish.

Chocolate Band-Aids (from Cost Plus in California) also do the trick (as long as your patient doesn't have a stomachache!).

Take Two Aspirins and a Flower, and Call Me in the A.M.
During flu season, I would go bank-rupt if I sent flowers to all of my friends who were down for the count . . . but one flower does not a bank account break. I take an empty aspirin bottle, fill it with water, add one 3-inch flower, and bring it with me on my visit. It gets the point across without making your banker ill. (You can also use an empty Band-Aid tin or anything else medicinal as your "vase.")

TLC
We all need a little tender love and care, no matter what's ailing us. If it's appropriate (meaning this is not your boss's mother-in-law twice removed), simply give your patients a blank check for some TLC. Let them tell you what it is they need and then fulfill those needs.

Ye Good Ol' Get-Well Basket
A basket can be customized to suit any personality prescription. And the goodies don't have to be housed in a basket. How about a tissue box for a cold . . . an apple crate for apples . . . a heating pad for a lousy back, and so on?

A Miserable Cold Basket Chicken soup, a book on tape, moisturizing tissues, aloe for the tender skin around the nose, magazines, and dry shampoo (always a lifesaver, it's called Psssst and costs about $4.99 in large drugstore chains).

A Lousy Back Basket A cell phone (even if it's on loan), tons of reading material, a video from your library, a nightshirt that's easy to change into, and once again, Psssst.

An Operation Basket A writing journal and pen, cocoa butter to prevent scarring, a book on tape, a neck-support pillow, cozy new socks, and, of course, Psssst.

An Apple a Day Basket Buffed (shiny) apples, apple-mint tea, apple marmalade, dried apples, and apple-flavored lozenges.

A Dr. Feel Good Basket Customize a basket that makes your sensational sickie feel good.

- If he loves racing, put in an OTB bet and a racing form
- If she loves jewelry, add a bead-making kit.
- If it's Gummi Bears that will help the hurt, fill the basket.

Food for Thought The late **Gilda Radner** used to make dozens of delicious homemade cookies for her friends and coworkers when they were under the weather. If you have a specialty of the house, you don't always need a special occasion in order to share it. Surprise those in your world with a homemade gift for no reason.

Long-Distance Takeout I think about food all the time, but when I'm as sick as a dog, I just can't bother. For the last 15 years, I've lived 1,500 miles away from my mom . . . but when I'm down for the count, my mom lets her credit card do the walking. She is there in spirit and nutrition. Even if you don't live in a metropolitan area, most local restaurants will accept a long-distance credit card charge. If you beg nicely, you can sometimes even get a busboy to deliver it. An incredible edible!

It's a Newborn

You've had nine months to prepare for this arrival, so you really shouldn't have labor pains deciding on the gift . . . but if you do, let's start with the basics.

A Birthday Cake

Yeah, this new kid on the block just had a birthday . . . so bake it or buy it, and bring it to the hospital.

Nonfat Birthday Cake

I am not implying that babies should be weight-conscious, but this cake is made out of diapers. This little confection was delivered to baby #3 in the **Warren Beatty/Annette Bening** household.

- **Buy your favorite brand of disposable newborn diapers. Leaving the first one folded, roll it like a jelly roll, so it forms the center of the cake.**

- **With the plastic facing the outside, wrap each consecutive diaper (about 12 of them) around the next, until it starts to look like a cake.**

🔍 Use straight pins to keep this pastry intact.

🔍 Add some pink or blue candles in the creases, and bon appétit. If you can get your hands on a bakery box for this treat, cut me a piece.

IOU What new parents really need is something we can't buy . . . time. But you can make some. Present your gift in the form of an IOU. Decide how many hours or chores you would like to donate to this new family; for example, baby-sit, grocery shop, cook dinner every Tuesday. Put it in writing and give it a family seal of approval. They may even make you an honorary godparent!

Piggy Bank Open a savings account in the baby's name, with you as the trustee. Contribute to this account for birthdays and holidays until the baby is all grown up. When the baby is an adult, that little piggy can go straight to the bank.

Mother's Day Sometimes during this hectic, wonderful time, all of us focus on the baby. But I love to get a little something for one of the people responsible for this blessed event . . . Mom. Since I am a positive thinker, I enjoy giving a couple of pairs of sexy panties to her, knowing that she will be able to squeeze into them in no time! Dad likes this too. . . .

Eye Bag Rescue Since both Mom and Dad will be up all night for at least the next two years, it's helpful to give them chamomile tea bags (which calm and soothe eye bags when used as compresses).

Pacifying Siblings

If you are visiting the newborn with gifts in tow, make sure you bring a little something to pacify his or her sister and brother. Even if it's just a lolly, it will help to distract them from all of the attention that the squiggly little crying thing is getting.

Diaper Doodles

If you would like to acknowledge the birth without giving a gift, get out some of your colored markers and write your note on the plastic side of the diaper. Stuff it in an envelope and you're done.

Diaper Decorating

I saw this next little number in a ritzy store in Beverly Hills for $75. It's a Hollywood baby best-seller. Guess what? We can do it for $3.98!

1. Buy a package of infant disposable diapers and a laundry marker.

2. On each diaper, write the baby's name multiple times on the bias. Don't worry if you don't have good handwriting.

3. Another option is to buy an ink stamp and pad that correspond to the parents' interests; for example, if they are sailors, stamp multiple sailboat images on the diaper in pink or blue ink. If they are into the stock market, alternate bulls and bears. If they are staunch Republicans, do an elephant motif.

Don't forget: this gift is disposable!

Baby BOTHER

Triple Threat

When visiting the tiny tot, snap a picture with your camera. Then quietly ask the grandparents for a baby picture of both Mom and Dad. Find a triple picture frame, and presto! This family has been framed.

The 21 Club Keepsake

This legendary New York establishment has recently discontinued a wonderful idea due to lack of space, but you can resurrect it in your own community. When a baby was born, a well-wisher would purchase a bottle of wine at the club that would be kept in the wine cellar until the baby turned 21. He or she would then come to the restaurant and toast the milestone. If there is an established restaurant in your hometown, perhaps the management could keep this tradition going, or you could simply keep the wine in the back of your closet for 21 years. After all, it's not getting older, it's getting better. (I can't believe I wrote that!)

Be Still My Heart

Multiple Grammy-winner **Lauryn Hill** and TV's morning sweetheart **Katie Couric** are both fans of jewelry designer Jeffrey Robert. The originator of the MicroCord, he now has added a floating diamond ring to his collection. (How do you say "to die for!"?) It can wind up on your finger (or the finger of someone you love) by calling Neiman Marcus or by visiting www.neimanmarcus.com.

Charmed, I'm Sure

Baby BOTHER

Guess what?! They're back! Not Milli Vanilli, but charm bracelets. When a baby girl is born, write a note to her, committing yourself to 21 charms for each coming birthday. This is a charming way to promise to know this wonderful little life.

Wells-Ware

Wells-Ware takes your own personal photographs, letters, postcards—any items that hold sentimental value—reduces and reshoots them, and places them into silver-framed glass charms. Wells-Ware will then turn these memories into a completely personal charm bracelet or necklace. **Oprah Winfrey**, **Julia Roberts**, **Spike Lee**, **Julianna Margulies**, and **Sting** are just a handful of celebrities who are already wearing Wells-Ware. Call 888-90-WELLS, or check out their "charming" Website (www.wellsware.com) for more information.

Kisses and Huggys

Many a celebrity earlobe has been "hugged" by these "wear any time, any place" silver-tone pavé earrings. J.J. Designs (310-393-7527), a gem of a boutique in Santa Monica, California, can't keep enough on the shelves. (Perhaps it's because they only cost $48!) Lord knows this isn't the only fake thing in Hollywood!

A Tree Grows Anywhere

When a child is born, plant a young tree in his or her honor, and watch them both grow. You just have to hope that the parents don't move away!

One Night Only

How many times have you gone to someone's home for dinner with a bottle of wine in a paper bag? It's a nice thought, but it's time for us to get out of that redundant rut. Your hosts change the meal every time you join them, so shouldn't you vary the gift, or at least enhance it?

Baby BOTHER

Stop Whining!

Okay, since bringing that nice bottle, or even a mediocre bottle, is typical, let's *"bother"* a bit, shall we? Stick with me as we dry a few dozen roses, and you'll understand why. (Of course, fresh flowers work just as well.) Whenever I am lucky enough to receive roses or I buy them "cheaply" for myself, I admire them for a day and while they are still partially open, I apologize to them, take each one out of the water, and snip an inch off the stem. I then turn them upside down and Scotch-tape the stems. I store them in an out-of-the-way dry place, such as a garage, a closet, or a laundry room. Once they are dry, I remove the tape, spray the flowers with hair spray, and store them indefinitely.

When I'm invited to someone's home at the last minute, I grab a bottle of wine and attach four or five dried roses to the bottle with one simple strand of raffia, cord, or ribbon.

The "Days of Wine and Roses" presentation (as I like to refer to it) takes about five minutes and is definitely worth the bother.

Finished Flowers

Don't get me wrong: flowers are always fabulous, but often the flowers you bring remain in their paper, in the corner of the kitchen, because the busy hostess has no time to put them in water. So, don't only bring the buds . . . bring the water too.

We're not talkin' an expensive vase. Have fun! Put them in a tennis ball can, a jar, a cookie tin, a bottle—anything that will keep them fresh and alive for the festivities.

Meal With an After Taste

I love gifts that keep giving, and magazine subscriptions always hit the spot. If your host is already a subscriber, don't worry: the amount of time can be extended. Bring one issue to the party, with a ribbon around it and a note that explains your ingenuity. You'll be amazed by how many different kinds of mags are out there now—from fly-fishing to frying fish.

Disposable Prez

No . . . this is not a political statement! Bringing a disposable camera as your gift to any shindig can be a picture-perfect present for your hosts. I am often the victim of low battery power and lack of film . . . but these guys are sure shots. And if you want to guarantee another invitation, you can take back the camera at the end of the event and have the pictures developed for your hosts.

Sinatra

Giving the gift of music changes people's lives. I find Sinatra to be multigenerational but, of course, personalize your purchase to the taste of your host. Usually, you can't go wrong with Frankie unless . . . you are one of his ex-wives!

"Wick"ed Gift

Candles—any shape, any size, any time—are always welcome. But a little extra knowledge never hurt anyone. I always wrap candles with a little ice tray. Yes, I get weird reactions, until the host reads my note. It explains that placing an ice cube over unwanted, dried candle wax lifts it right up. It's a miraculous problem solver.

Marvelous Miscellaneous

These ideas don't need an occasion. They're just fun and inexpensive "you-shouldn't-haves."

Geographically Desirable

In the FedEx world we live in, ordering a dozen stone crabs from Joe's in Miami is only a phone call away. But it's so much more meaningful to me when a friend takes the time and makes the effort to bring back items he or she can only buy outside of my area code or even country code. Here's a list of some of my personal long-distance favorites.

Detroit, MI	Vernor's Ginger Ale
Providence, RI	Coffee Syrup
Monterey, CA	Carmel Dark Brew Beer
Albuquerque, NM	a jug of Territorial House Salsa

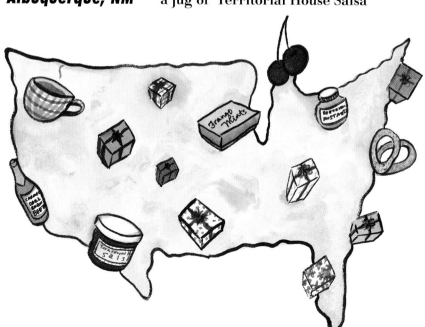

Chicago, IL	Brother's Root Beer and Frango Chocolates
Cleveland, OH	Bertrum Mustard
Travers City, MI	Anything Cherry
Brooklyn, NY	Peter Luger's Steak Sauce
London, England	Original Caramel Cadbury Bars (no, they don't sell them here)
Paris, France	Ellnet Hair Spray
Los Angeles, CA	Coffee Bean and Tea Leaf
Brookline, MA	Golden Temple Lobster Sauce
Philadelphia, PA	Sergeant's Pretzels (When bringing these back, make sure to keep them in the trunk, or they'll never make it past Exit 13 on the New Jersey Turnpike!)

Start adding your own goodies to this list . . . and get ready for some long-distance smiles.

Pick Me Ups
Whether your little sad sack is 8 or 80—when someone is having a bad day, offer up a split second of kindness. Even one chocolate kiss and a note can help move the clouds away.

For a permanent chocolate kiss . . . Celebration Fantastic (1-800-CELEBRATE) offers silver- and gold-painted porcelain boxes. Everlasting love at $18 each.

Nice and Naughty Notes

A surprise note in a lunch box, under a pillow, in a briefcase, in a suit pocket, on a desk, or in a suitcase provides special moments. When writing to kids, it's fun to use a crayon. (Just don't mix up the cute-and-cuddly note you write to your seven-year-old with the burning desire message you just scripted for your hubby!)

Cherry Pie

What do **Gwyneth Paltrow**, **Sharon Stone**, **Winona Ryder**, **Jennifer Aniston**, and **Bette Midler** all have in common? Cherry Pie, of course. No, not the dessert, but their delicious 100% cotton cherry-patterned pj's.

Sharon Stone has such pleasant dreams while wearing hers that she has the company send her their newest designs monthly. If you want a piece of the pie, simple call Cherry Pie at 310-204-6699.

Filling Your Shoe

I've found fabulous miniature shoes at a craft store, but you can use doll shoes or even a shoe from the person you want to surprise if you have access. When someone is moving away, leaving a job, or just feeling unworthy, simply fill the shoe with candy or chocolate kisses. The sentiment is "no one can fill your shoes"—a simple idea with deep implications. Just the Right Shoe manufactures the greatest collection of rightly priced miniature shoes I've ever seen. In more than 78 designs, these little items are true works of art. They are sold at more than 12,000 retailers worldwide. Visit their website to find one near you. If the shoe fits, order it! www.willitts.com, 707-778-7211. They also sell miniature chairs that are sooo cute they will melt your heart.

Baby BOTHER

Fortune 500

Here's a gift that's guaranteed not to cost you a fortune! Sun Golden Cookies Corp. (212-431-9695), in lower Manhattan, makes personalized fortune cookies that are yours for the asking. You can compose your own words of wisdom, and the fabulous fortune makers at Sun will insert them into the cookies! Fifteen dollars will get you 100 cookies . . . and for an extra $5, the "golden ones" will individually wrap 'em for your eating pleasure.

The World's Greatest Thank-You Note

I carry a throwaway camera everywhere I go, including in my fancy-schmancy evening bags. If I'm at a dinner party, dining as someone's guest in a restaurant, at a wedding, or if someone simply does something nice for me, I try to get one shot that captures the moment. I include the developed picture in the thank-you note, and I always, always, always put it in a frame. It becomes so much more meaningful when it's framed and won't wind up all squished in the bottom of a pocketbook or drawer.

🔍 **I also love *chocolate mini rolls of film* from California's Cost Plus chain. They fit in standard envelopes and can be used for thanking folks for "picture-perfect evenings"!**

911 Emergency Gifts

When you've got a lot of heart but not a lot of time!

Just the Ticket

Whoever said that gift certificates are impersonal obviously never visited GiftCertificates.com. This is one-stop shopping at its finest, with over 200 stores in 14 categories to choose from. Simply choose a store from their extensive list, select the appropriate amount for your gift certificate, choose a greeting card and gift wrap, and you're done!

May I Have the Envelope Please?

RedEnvelope.com offers a variety of "911 gifts," for those last-minute Oopsies. . . . Order your gift by midnight EST, and it can arrive the next morning! And if you're wondering where exactly the "red envelope" comes into play, just look outside your door tomorrow morning—if you've ordered—you'll understand.

Don't Surf and Drive

At wine.com, you can not only order the luscious liquid, you can also learn about the folks who made it.

Guaranteed Gifts

Whether you have $5 to spend or $5,000, read on. . . . For years, I have collected unique gift sources that I truly treasure. Many of these (and the folks associated with them) are true gems. There will be no returns if you choose any one of these items.

Bellyache Cove Crafters

Come on, you've gotta love the name of this Hamilton, Massachusetts, dream factory (978-525-4870). Kelli Healey Petri makes copper cookie cutters from your child's hand print. The child's name, age, and a message can be engraved on the side. This is such a historic gift for Mother's Day, Father's Day, christenings, and birthdays. It costs $20 plus shipping and handling. Kelly can also craft company logos, children's profiles, or any sketch into a cookie cutter. Checks only, please.

Life Is Just a Bowl & Wishbone Wishes

Leigh Hamilton, the owner of Hamilton Galleries in L.A., knows how to dress her salad (only kidding). She represents Tamara Hensick, a unique artist who has designed a whimsical, wonderfully affordable, sterling silver wishbone. It is so affordable and should bring good luck to any occasion. Hensick also designed a sterling "cherry" to remind us that life is indeed a bowl of cherries, and a sterling leaf to turn over at any time for any reason. This good karma will cost you $20 for the small wishbone, $56 for the cherry, and $88 for the leaf. Call 310-859-7824. All are designed with a positive philosophy. Whenever I give the cherry as a gift, I include it in a little basket of real cherries. (If they are not in season, I substitute wooden ones!)

Daisy 28

Tucked into a gritty side street of New York City's wholesale flower district is Soon Ok Kim, a designer who magically transforms dried flowers into couture 13-inch mannequins. These works of art can be done in a bridal theme, as French rose ladies, or in any lavish designs your imagination desires. They range from $65 to $105 and can be shipped all around the world. If they are damaged in transit, Daisy 28 (212-268-7231) will replace the item. With credit card in hand, run to the Web (www.daisy28.com).

There's No Place Like Home

If you love the illustrations in this book as much as I do, and you love your home, how about a little merger? The artful Marian Nixon (773-588-8640) will paint a beautiful original watercolor of your home from a photograph. This is a great surprise house-warming gift and a thoughtful, sentimental present when you are leaving a house. This beautiful, priceless memory starts at $250.

Lifesavers You can get this gift for that person in your life who always seems to throw you the buoy when you are in deep water. There are three different prices: $5, $25, or $320, depending on what you include.

- Simply fill a gift bag with multicolored ribbons and include packages of Lifesaver candies with a note that champions *your* lifesaver.

- Add to the bag a wonderful hand-painted porcelain keepsake that is a replica of the Nabisco packages ($24.95 in the Potpourri catalog; 800-688-8051).

- And to add a little extravagant elegance to the proceedings . . . *über* handbag designer Judith Leiber offers a dazzling, bejeweled pillbox—in the form of a Lifesavers package ($320 in upscale department stores or in Judith Leiber shops). All three of these gift bags are lifesavers.

The Write Stationery These papers put stars in the eyes of **George Lucas**. He is a big fan of Melissa Wood and Amy Alexander from Barrington, Illinois (847-382-8681). Their unique hand-painted doodles have graced the writing desk of this box-office giant, among other discerning buyers. Some of their specialty papers include portraits of birthday cakes, dachshunds, pocketbooks, and place settings. Their designs are whimsical winners. Call for a catalog and prepare to swoon.

Hanky-Panky

Barbara Goodfriend (609-667-6454) is totally on the level with her magnificent handmade monogrammed handkerchiefs. They are crafted in Maderia, Spain, and are truly one of a kind. Too beautiful to ever really use, these pima cotton gems will bring your initials to a new level of art—they are cut out within the fabric. I am thinking of framing the ones that I received.

Diamond Bouquet

Custom jewelry designer Sherri Miller (212-944-2153) planted an idea that has blossomed onto many a lapel. She's done a variety of 1-inch flower pins that are adorable when worn solo but form a bountiful bouquet on a blouse or dress when grouped together. They range from $60 to $500, depending on what materials you choose: sterling silver and cubic zirconias, 18-karat gold and gemstones, and white gold with diamonds. You can mix and match or even buy one for each occasion. It makes me wanna have birthdays! (Did I say that?)

Welcome Home

The Sweet Tooth in Miami, Florida (305-682-1400), makes the sweetest housewarming gift: a chocolate house, 4 inches by 1½ inches, with the name of the new tenants written on the roof, packed in pretty cellophane. It costs much less than your mortgage—just $3 per house! They will ship all over the United States but only through FedEx.

Joy to the World

Joy Dennison, the owner of this magical emporium (877-846-6890), believes that her hand-designed cookies are a special blessing. And she is right. She began her business with gorgeous gingerbread boys and now designs just about anything. There is no minimum order, and each little work of art is priced by weight.

Romantic Ceramic

Deirdre Schwartz comes from London but parks her kiln in Santa Monica, California (310-319-0074). She does a personalized heart-shaped graffiti plate for $40. The texture looks like a brick wall with the couple's initials seemingly spray-painted onto it, inside a heart. It's terrific! Her other pièce de résistance is her couple platter—a fantabulous wedding or anniversary gift. It celebrates 200 famous duos, such as Romeo and Juliet, Bogie and Bacall, Monica and Bill, and comes with about 25 personal couplets that are meaningful to the couple. All of these are etched onto the plate, which is then glazed. At $125 plus shipping and handling, it's a real bargain. Deirdre accepts personal checks, and you'll want to give her your personal compliments. I recently gave the plate as a wedding gift to the president of a studio, and he confessed that it was his favorite.

Vosges Haut Chocolate

It's definitely not your dad's Hershey bar. The mission statement of this Chicago company (777-772-5346) is to position itself as an innovator delivering globally conscious, contemporary truffles. Delicate attention goes into every spice, flower, and chocolate and into creating unique combinations: chocolate infused with ginger and wasabi; chocolate and coconut curry; and chocolate, cream, and Hungarian paprika. You're grimmacing, but these combos are delicious. Paramount Pictures gave these confections to **Kelsey Grammer** for his birthday. A ¼-pound box is $16, but the truffles are sold individually for $1.60 and packaged in Chinese takeout containers—chopsticks not included.

Creative Chocolates of Vermont

The cold weather in Essex Junction, Vermont, certainly does not freeze the creativity of Peg McGowan (802-879-7330): she delights in offering her unusual chocolate creations. Trust me . . . I'm not exaggerating. How about a TV dinner featuring a chocolate ham, veggies, potatoes, and dessert? A spaghetti dinner with fudge meatballs? Peanut butter pancakes with fudge centers? And, of course, a chocolate cheeseburger with all the fixins. These edibles range from $7.75 to $8.50. If you know someone who is renovating his or her home and needs a pick-me-up, how about a real paint can filled with chocolate tools and a paint roller filled with M&M's ($17)? Peg also does a chocolate toilet seat cover, but I've yet to send one. She is flush with ideas!

Ravioli Royalty

No, Queen Elizabeth does not eat these, but to me, anything chocolate is to the manner born. The Gevalia catalog (800-438-2542) serves up white chocolate in the shape of ravioli, stuffed with dark chocolate, ground hazelnuts, and rum. Eleven of these wonders come in a gift box for $24.95 (www.gevalia.com).

Nonnie's Traditional Southern

When my buddy Kristina told me about Nonnie (800-664-0919 or www.nonniestraditional) many years ago, I felt like it was our cherished little secret, but lo and behold, *In Style* (one of my favorite magazines) outed Nonnie right before the millennium. But in case you missed that issue, I must share this gem. Nonnie takes individual hatboxes and covers them with magnificent fabrics. Inside is the most delicious espresso-laced chocolate pound cake (or perfectly plain) with fresh flowers in the center. There is also a fabulous brooch as the closure. For bundles of joy, Nonnie does the hatbox in pink or blue silk, with hand-sewn ceramic blocks that spell out the baby's name. The hatboxes are wrapped in satin and gingham with posy-embroidered bows. These one-of-a-kind beauties range from $65 to $125. Credit cards are gladly accepted, and the hatbox arrives in perfect condition. Many superstars have ordered these incredible edibles, but Nonnie keeps their identities under her hat.

Moosie Wrappers

This company, based in Hillard, Ohio (614-876-8723), makes custom-wrapped chocolate bars that are deliciously creative. They offer personalized bars for any occasion, but what can't be beat are their baby announcements, which include family ingredients, the net weight of the baby, and, of course, the claim "manufactured with love" from the baby's parents. The wrappers are 75 cents each, but they are so highly personalized that they are actually priceless.

Chocolate Geography

For $10, you can own real estate in a large variety of countries, states, cities, and mountain ranges . . . but did I mention that it would be edible? Topo Chocolate (800-779-8985) makes unusual maps out of the good stuff of over 100 locations—a great cheap way to travel (www.topochocolate.com).

Trompe L'oeil Filled With Joy

Here's the good news: you can keep your van Goghs and Picassos and even your cut-velvet montage of Elvis. When I received this picture-perfect present, I literally jumped in the air. Creative director and style connoisseur Lynn Huberman (877-771-0834) offers a highly personalized painting of trompe l'oeil shelves filled with the keepsakes and history of your life. (Now, in case your French is rusty, trompe l'oeil is a method of painting in which the subject is done with 3D realism). If it's a surprise wedding gift, it could include re-creations of a framed picture of the couple, a cork from their favorite champagne, a baseball cap from their favorite team, a scrunchie from her ponytail, a bottle of hot sauce from the Mexican restaurant where they met . . . anything from the past can be frozen in time for the future. I was lucky enough to have received my painting for my 30th birthday, but it is also a fantastic anniversary gift. These moments in time can be found hanging in many a celebrity study, but Lynn has a strict confidentiality code. You'll definitely want to reach out and touch. You can also touch her Website (www.ivyhillbunch.com).

Breakable ... Makable ... and Sensational

The talented family of artists who form Rubino's Art Village (914-482-3573) are from the isle of Capri in Italy, but now make their magic in Jeffersonville, New York. Their work has been commissioned twice by the pope, as well as by the Metropolitan Museum of Art. Now they can be commissioned by you. Besides their line of magnificent ceramics, their custom work is incredible. If you dream it, they can scheme it. From a dog bowl for your Fido, to kitchen tiles that re-create the pattern of your chair fabric, to a personalized baby bottle for your niece, to 500 ceramic business cards to publicize that you've moved your office. I adore a $275 wine carafe with matching goblets and tray on which they paint the person's name. They accept compliments as well as credit cards. This is a family business run by remarkable folk.

You Can Adopt a Piece of Central Park

The best seat in New York is Central Park's conservatory program, "Adopt a Bench" (212-310-6600), which ensures that this green jewel is maintained meticulously. Your tax-deductible dollars enable you to personalize a specific bench in the name of anything you desire. The bench you choose is engraved with a plaque of 40 letters. Some are adopted by a group in honor of a person, place, or shared experience. ABC anchorman **Peter Jennings** and his bride received a bench as a wedding present. **Bill Cosby** also has a permanent seat in sylvan splendor. There are over 8,000 to choose from, and you get to select your desired setting. For 5,000 tax-deductible dollars, I personally think it should come with a cushion . . . but it is a grand gift. So don't just sit there—go out and get a bank loan.

I hope that we've included just about every occasion and every type of person in your life, but I know we've left out a very important person . . . you! Let me let you in on a little personal secret: my birthday is August 6, and on the sixth of every month, I buy myself a little something . . . and here's the embarrassing part. I even have it gift wrapped! While you're so busy enhancing everyone else's life, don't forget to give to the giver.

You are now Present and Accounted For!

You're Invited!
Sam's Birthday
April 20th, 8pm
RSVP 555-1234

Parties R Us

An average Hollywood premiere bash can cost a studio up to $5 million. And after a while, they all start to look alike! (Yeah, gorgeous!) But if you haven't budgeted that much in your party piggy bank, read on, because I know that **you have the ability to become a perfect party planner.** You see, I have a foolproof "trick" up my sleeve that will help you create any conceivable celebration. But before we start the trickery, here are some Tinseltown touches to whet your appetite! One of the best soirees I've ever been to involved **Frank Sinatra**, a clove of garlic, and apron strings. Okay, I'll explain. Sinatra not only had a way with a song but also knew his way around the kitchen. When he first began to market his own brand of pasta sauces, he invited about 15 members of the press to cook along with him. The invitation was hand-written on an apron, the centerpieces were dried pasta instead of flowers, my place card had my name on it, along with the recipe, and *La traviata* was blaring through the stereo speakers! At the end of the evening, every guest was given Frank's new cookbook and spaghetti tongs to take home.

Sure, it was a kick that this was Sinatra's party, but even if the host had been your Uncle Vinny, all the elements were in place for a great evening. Thought and creativity were needed to make the occasion special, not 5 million bucks. The evening had a focus—a theme that was carried out involving small inexpensive touches, from the invitations, to the centerpieces, to the parting gifts.

The **Star Wars: Episode I—The Phantom Menace** *premiere* served food from another galaxy: Trade Federation tacos and tamales, Darth dogs, and Jar Jar Binks burgers—and to satisfy the sweet tooth, Obi's Wan-derful desserts with solar sundaes, Wookie cookies, and Amidala's chocolate brownie pudding. What's in a name? A lot.

Tomorrow Never Dies, the James Bond thriller starring **Pierce Brosnan**, had a thrilling premiere party. The invitations were telegrams with cryptic information about where the party was being held, which made you feel as if you were a spy decoding the information. And, of course, every martini was served shaken—not stirred.

The **Blues Brothers 2000** *premiere at the Cannes Film Festival* got everyone in a festive mood by handing out fedoras and sunglasses as the guests first arrived. It's a great idea to think of a similar gimmick to get your own party going right from the start.

Runaway Bride, starring **Julia Roberts** and **Richard Gere**, did not do runaway business at the box office, but the premiere party was critically acclaimed. First-nighters were feted at an L.A. museum, where the film's small town of Hale, Maryland, was re-created. Buffet tables became part of the scenery, including the town's bridal shop, beauty parlor, diner, and hardware store. And for a picture-perfect souvenir of the evening, guests had their photos snapped behind a six-tiered wedding cake "prop," trimmed with real frosting.

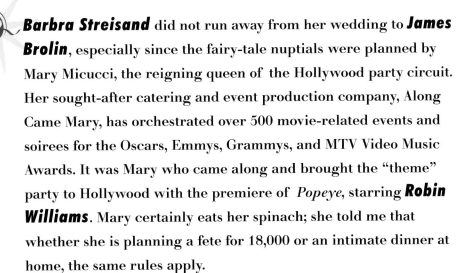

Barbra Streisand did not run away from her wedding to ***James Brolin***, especially since the fairy-tale nuptials were planned by Mary Micucci, the reigning queen of the Hollywood party circuit. Her sought-after catering and event production company, Along Came Mary, has orchestrated over 500 movie-related events and soirees for the Oscars, Emmys, Grammys, and MTV Video Music Awards. It was Mary who came along and brought the "theme" party to Hollywood with the premiere of *Popeye*, starring ***Robin Williams***. Mary certainly eats her spinach; she told me that whether she is planning a fete for 18,000 or an intimate dinner at home, the same rules apply.

- Be excited and feel that whatever you're doing is special and important.

- Use that energy to visualize what you want to accomplish.

- Be organized: make lists and stay within your budget.

- Don't stress over money. If you want to hire help and you can't afford it, then buy your groceries from a discount warehouse to free up some dough.

The magnificent Mary is hired not only because of her limitless talent and boundless energy but also because she brings the gift of passion to every party.

Now all this Hollywood hash is heavenly . . . but how can it help you? Well the trick is in the ***"trick."*** You see, every time you sit down to plan a party, think of the word "trick," making sure all of your bases are covered.

T = Theme

R = Refreshments

I = Invitations

C = Centerpieces and Creative Eye Candy (nonedible)

K = Kudos (that you will receive)

Okay . . . now let's make some party magic out of the "*trick*." At first, it may seem like a lot of work, but once you get the hang of it, you won't leave home without it.

Theme

You don't have to reinvent the wheel every time you plan a shindig. But if you keep repeating the same ideas, celebrations can get stale. To avoid this, try this simple exercise. Take a blank piece of paper and write the purpose of your party on the top line. For instance, "Bonnie's Baby Shower." Now write down five things that you can think of regarding Bonnie's Baby Shower. I know that you might be running out of ideas by #5, but just let your mind expand, even if some of your ideas are weak (a nice way of saying "not so good"). Now, walk away and revisit your list a little later in the day . . . and from among those five ideas, your theme will become clear.

Example: Bonnie's Baby Shower

1 **Special Delivery**

2 **Stork Club**

3 **Mommy Dearest**

4 **Pretty in Pink**

5 **Under Construction**

Once you commit to your theme, the rest of the **"trick"** just seems to fall into place. For this imaginary occasion, I'm going to choose—drum-roll, please—"Pretty in Pink," because I think it can act as a spring-board for ideas.

Refreshments

"Food for Thought" should be your recipe guide when planning your party eats. Of course, not every morsel can correlate to your theme, but you'll be surprised by what you can come up with when you are working with one basic concept. Remember, just a couple of related items can generate an all-encompassing feeling.

Since our sample theme is "Pretty in Pink," I would serve a lunch that is mostly pink. That doesn't mean I add food coloring to everything or splash Rit dye everywhere. Relating your food to your theme just takes a little ingenuity.

🔍 **Cold smoked salmon**

🔍 **Salmon mousse**

🔍 Assorted **baby lettuces** with **raspberry vinaigrette**

🔍 **Stork cake** with pink chiffon icing

Food for Thought

Serve pink rum punch in baby bottles for foolproof party pleasers. Buy regular-size baby bottles in a discount store and you've got a fun and creative way to toast the mother-to-be! (Since alcohol is not recommended for expectant moms, virgin pink punch will do just fine!) And if you're not such a good cook, you can have Pepto-Bismol on hand . . . the color matches your theme! (Just kidding!)

Invitations

Tom Hanks, Oprah Winfrey, and **Robin Williams** are smart enough to hire Creative Intelligence in L.A. for their party invitation needs. This company specializes in custom finery, from pop-up fantasies to leather-bound corporate invites (313-936-9009). I know this might sound obvious, but please remember that invites need to be inviting—duh! They set the whole tone for the shindig. So put your best foot forward by putting some thought and effort into this preparty appe-teaser.

In this prefab world we live in, it is comforting for invites to seem "custom-made" even if they are not. It's okay to go the "store-bought" way . . . that's great, but please doctor it up a bit.

- For our "Pretty in Pink" theme, buy some inexpensive pink diaper pins and attach one to each invitation to instantly make it more personal.

- Take your store-bought invite and roll it up like a scroll. Now slip it into the ring of a pink pacifier and stuff it into your envelope—an adorable presentation in just 40 seconds!

- Use a pink marker to write all of your party patter on a small plastic diaper. Fold the diaper (attach a diaper pin if you like), pop in an envelope, and you have done your "duty."

- Buy small plastic baby bottles at a discount store. Fill them with pink jelly beans and use a laundry marker to write all the party information on the bottle. If you're in the mood, tie pink curling ribbon around the rim of the bottle.

Baby BOTHER

Special Delivery Get a baby picture of the mother-to-be. Photocopy it and place it in an inexpensive frame. Mail this special delivery out to the partygoers with all your party info on the back of the frame. You'll make the stork proud!

Big BOTHER

"Voice Mail" If the baby-to-be has a sibling, have that child invite the guests on an audiocassette: the more "raw," the more adorable. Don't expect a professional radio announcer, 'cuz you ain't gonna get it, but you will get unforgettable family history.

Centerpieces and Creative Eye Candy

If you've ever gone to a dinner party and proclaimed how lovely the vase with the $2.98 grocery store-bought carnations are, wait till you get a load of this section. I don't have a long-standing grudge against carnations, and I do adore cheap price tags, but your centerpiece should not be an afterthought. It is the focal point of the whole shebang. To help you brainstorm and get out of your centerpiece rut, come into my think tank.

Think *conversation piece*

Think *humor*

Think *grand and glorious*

Think *earthy and edible*

One of these elements *should* help jump-start your creative thinking process. . . .

At a recent Academy Awards ceremony, the Governor's Ball took place adjacent to where the Oscars were telecast. The celebrities left their seats and entered an auditorium decorated with over $1 million worth of flowers. However, the flowers on the tables remained simple and elegant. Each place setting had a cobalt blue vase (which I've seen a near-identical replica of at Pottery Barn for $8.95) with a single flower in it. Hey, if you were sitting across the table from **Brad Pitt**, you wouldn't want your view to be blocked either! I don't think that Brad Pitt will be attending our sample "Pretty in Pink" baby shower . . . but dry those tears, because life goes on, and we still have to come up with some great centerpiece ideas. Referring back to the think tank, "conversation piece" and "humor" seem to be the categories that would fit this type of occasion.

- **Blue (or Pink) Bonnet:** Put a baby's bonnet upside down on the table and stuff it halfway with tissue paper to give it shape. Then fill it with Hershey's kisses or lollies.

- **Party Animal:** Seat a teddy bear (or another stuffed animal with a paw) at the center of the table. Choose a single flower. Push a straight pin through the stem of the flower into the animal, making it look like he or she is holding the bloom. For animal lovers everywhere: this is not painful!

- **Pail Pink:** Fill a diaper pail with daisies. This is more aesthetically pleasing than a simple vase of pink carnations.

🔍 **Pampering:** Empty the contents of a Pampers box (or any disposable diaper package). Place a flower-filled vase inside the box. (The vase should be no taller than the top of the box or you will ruin the magical effect.)

🔍 **Starry-eyed Stroller:** Fill a small doll carriage with pink or blue flowers.

Baby BOTHER

A versatile centerpiece that always gets rave reviews is a little number that I call **"Let Them Eat Cake."** And since our theme is somewhat related to a "birth" day, this floral birthday cake will hit the spot.

1 Buy a round piece of floral Styrofoam.

2 Soak it in water for one minute.

3 Cut the flowers of your choice to a height of one inch.

4 Place them around the sides of the mold, overlapping them so that no Styrofoam is showing.

5 Do the same on the top.

6 Place your flower cake on a cake plate.

7 Add a knife as an accessory.

Enjoy. It contains no calories!

Passing on the Party There was a time in the greedy '80s when floral centerpieces were so large, even your robust Aunt Velma couldn't manage to take them home. Extravagant money was spent on flowers that would surely wilt after a three-hour affair. Now that we're a bit older and wiser, a centerpiece can live on and serve a greater purpose. After the last dance has been danced, many folks donate their floral arrangements to hospitals. At a recent wedding, I saw centerpieces made out of canned goods, which were donated to a homeless shelter after the party. At a pediatric AIDS benefit on the Universal lot in Hollywood, menageries of stuffed animals were used as the centerpieces and later donated to the children's ward at Cedars Sinai Hospital.

Centerpieces and Creative Eye Candy

Natty napkin rings, perfect place cards, and other little sweet "tricks" that will make your party special are so easy to create and add so much to the mix.

Napkin Rings

- Wrap the napkin around a fork, knife, and spoon and fasten it with a pink or blue diaper pin.

- Slip the napkin through the ring of a pacifier.

- Kids' Band-Aids have wonderful designs. Wrap the silverware with a paper or cloth napkin and seal with a Band-Aid.

- Perhaps your Aunt Matilda knits.

If not, buy doll booties or baby booties. Wrap the fork, knife, and spoon in a napkin and tuck the bundle inside the bootie as far as it will go.

Place Cards

❧ Write the guest's name in kids' handwriting in pink crayon.

❧ Fill doll-size baby bottles with pink jelly beans and write the guest's name on the bottom.

Baby BOTHER **Finding Yourself** I love this. . . . Before the shindig, ask each guest for a baby picture of him- or herself. At each place setting, lean the picture against a glass or plate, or place each picture in an inexpensive frame. It's fun to watch the guests try to find themselves.

Baby BOTHER **Spelling Beads** String together baby bracelet beads to spell out a guest's first name. Punch two holes on either side of a plain place card or glue the beads to the card. You can also use your grown-up baby bracelets as napkin rings. Just tie them around your napkins.

At a recent Polygram Records' Grammy party at the New York Racquet and Tennis Club, the "red carpet" was out for every guest. The champagne was flowing, but what found some guests "seeing red" wasn't the bubbly—it was the bulbs! Colored red bulbs replaced the regular lighting, bathing the room in a red glow. You can do this easily at home. Buy colored bulbs at your local hardware store. Sometimes, I even replace a bulb or two during dinner (when I don't want people to see what I've made!). For our "Pretty in Pink" shower, pink bulbs will definitely add to the ambience.

Kudos

Congrats—it's a party! You have labored and given birth to a sensational shower!

Now that you've learned the "trick," let's try another. . . .

Theme: Good-bye Party: Barbara Goes to Paris

Remember . . . in order to tackle the theme, we need to do that simple exercise of writing down five related elements for our good-bye party. (Don't make a face—this exercise is much easier than doing sit-ups.) Okay . . . here goes.

1. Gay Paris (you can replace Paris with your friend's destination)
2. Bon Voyage (a tad obvious, but it would work)
3. Take Me Along
4. Barbara's Bistro (provided your friend's name is Barbara— and mine is)
5. French Kiss

Drumroll, please . . .

I'm going to choose **"Barbara's Bistro,"** because I think that it has loads of personal potential.

Refreshments

In my dream world, we are all five-star French chefs, but back here on Earth, it's not a sin to go to McDonald's, buy a couple of orders of French fries, reheat them in your microwave, and voilà . . . you immediately have French bistro fare! But fries do not a meal make. You could add tuna salad, egg salad, or crabmeat salad in the shape of the Eiffel Tower: you don't have to be an architect, just take off your rings and start molding your food on a flat surface. You did this in kindergarten and you can do it now.

If brunch is what you're after, there's always the proverbial croissant, and what about some flavored French toast? Just add a teaspoon of almond extract, grated orange rind, Grand Marnier, or Framboise liquer to your egg and milk batter and sauté as usual. This just in: you can also make French toast the day before.

Wave the Flag

This geographically desirable dessert is *sooo* easy. Bake a yellow sheet cake from a mix in a rectangular pan. Ice the whole cake with Cool Whip, or real whipped cream. (By the way, freezing your beaters before whipping helps add puff to your cream.)

🔍 **Divide the top of the cake into three sections.**

🔍 **Top the left third with raspberries or strawberries.**

🔍 **Leave the center white, and cover the right side with blueberries (if fresh berries are not in season drained, defrosted frozen ones will do).**

You now not only have a yummy dessert, but also just created the French flag. And if you have no time to bake, you can skip the cake layer, and just use the fruit and cram.

Food For Thought
Although I think it is swell to serve food that represents your theme, every once in a while opposites attract. If your guest of honor is going to be spending seven weeks in the Orient, he or she might have a yen for hot dogs, pizza, or bagels and lox instead of egg foo young! And you won't be hungry four hours later!

Invitations

Picture Postcards
Try to get your paws on some postcards from the place where your guest of honor is headed. Then just scribble your pertinent party patter, stamp, and send!

Marker Mania
Buy an appropriate invitation. Use red, white, and blue markers (the colors of the French flag) to fill in the information.

Booze Bottles Don't just collect frequent-flier miles; collect airplane mini liquor bottles (which can also be purchased at your local liquor store). Use the empty bottles as containers for your invitations. Stuff 'em, pop on the top, and ship 'em out. The results are intoxicating. Sometimes I pair the bottles with other travel props, such as a toy train or plane!

Baby BOTHER

An American in Paris This film can be found in most local video stores. Rent it, and photocopy the cover of the tape. Use the color copy as your invite and be sure to include all of the party particulars.

Baby BOTHER

"On the Menu" Bat those eyelashes and borrow a menu from your local French establishment. "Wite-Out" the restaurant's name and replace it with the name of the theme you've selected (in our case, "Barbara's Bistro"). Inside, write your party patter . . . for instance:

Plat du jour: One rare, juicy going-away party

Big BOTHER

Boarding Pass Find an old boarding pass and "Wite-Out" your personal information. Photocopy the empty form and fill in any information that pertains to your guests: name, gate/table #, and so on. No electronic tickets will be accepted here!

Centerpieces and Creative Eye Candy

Leaving on a Jet Plane
Fill a toy airplane with candy, dried fruits, or nuts. If you're diet-conscious, money can be used in place of candy. Sprinkle the coin currency of your destination around the table for a sparkling effect. Different modes of transportation, such as boats, trains, or cars, can be used to fit your bill.

Hats Off!
Borrow some berets from your Uncle Jacques. Stuff them with newspaper to keep their shape and place them in the center of each table.

Tricolor Stripes
Fill a tall glass vase with flowers. Tie a striped French neckerchief around the neck of the vase. *C'est magnifique!*

Cry Baby
Fill a bucket with salt water and place it at the center of the table, signifying the tears you'll shed when the person leaves.

Packing Pleasure
Take a small suitcase and prop up the top with unsharpened pencils (the pencils will not be visible). Fill the suitcase with plants such as trailing ivy. This centerpiece is a lovely alternative to carnations in a vase, and the airlines will never lose this piece of luggage.

Baby BOTHER

Chain Gang When friends announced that they were taking a bicycle trip to the south of France, I found a $6 wooden bicycle planter at Cost Plus in West Los Angeles for their going-away party. Naturally, I filled it with plants; unnaturally, I stopped at Home Depot and bought a few yards of what looked like bicycle chain. I had the store cut it (God forbid I should break a nail!) and used the chain to make napkin rings.

Creative Eye Candy

Place Cards

Luggage Tags Buy paper, plastic, or leather luggage tags (depending on your budget) and simply write the guest's name on the paper provided. Then attach the tags to the silverware, the napkins, or even the chairs.

Postcards Try to get your paws on some postcards from the place where your guest of honor is headed. Write each guest's name and address on the postcards and place them on the table. Not only do you get to decide who sits next to Aunt Bertha, but the guest of honor gets to keep the stamped cards, and you are guaranteed to get a "wish you were *here*" while she's *there!*

Foreign Currency Write the person's name on the coin with a thin-tip laundry marker. (Don't worry, your guest will still be able to use it to buy you something in return for throwing him or her such a nice going-away party.)

Place Mats Under each place setting, place a map of the guest of honor's destination or a brochure (which your friendly travel agent can get for you at no extra cost.)

Country Coordinated Buy inexpensive napkins (paper or fabric) that correspond to the country the person is going to: red and green for Italy, red and white for Canada, and so on. If you spill, at least you'll be color coordinated!

Big BOTHER

Coffee, Tea, and Pillows I found what looked like small airplane pillows at a discount fabric store on New York's Lower East Side. With a laundry marker, I wrote each guest's name on the pillowcases. Using double-sided tape, I then attached each pillow to the back of each chair. Clever, yet comfy!

Creative Ear Candy

An Edith Piaf or Charles Aznavour CD will fill the air with French flair. But don't worry . . . you don't need to lease a music library to set the mood. If you're looking to keep costs down, invest in just one CD. Play it at the very beginning of your fling, to establish your atmosphere.

Kudos *Merci Beaucoup!*

Theme: Wedding Shower: * Katie Ties the Knot *

I love this soiree because you can have as many "choices" in this arena as you can have husbands. To help you decide what the theme should be, focus your exercise on what kinds of gifts you want your bride-to-be to receive. For instance . . .

Honeymoon Shower
Gifts that the couple can use on their honeymoon! My, my, you have a dirty mind—I was thinking about a travel alarm clock.

Kitchen Shower
Naturally, items for the kitchen. We all know that food represents love, so what better time to bring the two together?

Round-the-Clock Shower

On the invitation, assign each guest a time of day and explain that the gift should correspond in some way to the time given. For instance: 7:30 A.M.—a coffee maker; 7:30 P.M.—a martini maker! (Here is a napkin ring I once used for a "round-the-clock" shower: a toy watch with a photocopy of the happy couple's picture.)

Bedroom Shower

There's more than lingerie in this category. Think about a Scrabble game to play in bed, fancy-schmancy water glasses for your nightstand, even bedtime stories.

Advise and Consent

Have each guest present the bride-to-be with advice on how to live "happily ever after." Counsel coming from a 14-year-old, a twice-divorced aunt, and a great-grandmother can be very entertaining.

Between the Sheets

Items that can be used between the ol' sheets, such as body lotion, lingerie, foot warmers . . . even condoms!

Something Old, New, Borrowed, Blue

Divide the guests into four groups. The first group brings something old as a gift, the second something new, the third something borrowed, the fourth something blue.

Extend the Theme to Your Table Setting:

An **Antique** Vase

filled with **New** flowers

Borrowed assorted plates

on a **Blue** tablecloth.

I know I've given you more than five, but I got carried away.

I'm going to go with "Kitchen shower," because, quite frankly . . .

I love to eat.

Refreshments

Here's where the whole kitchen sink comes into play. This field is pretty wide open. Let's start by involving your kitchen.

- Whether you're in a one-room apartment in Memphis, or a four-bedroom Tudor in Cleveland, start the party in the hallowed room known as "the kitchen." Serve drinks and some tidbits from your countertops.

- If there is a chef in your town who is a ham (I didn't say "who can make a ham") and who would like to make a few bucks on the side, invite him or her to play "show and tell" in your kitchen. He or she can cook for the guests and teach them while sautéing.

- Divide your guests into categories, and ask each partygoer to bring her specialty of the house (along with the recipe on an 8 x 10 index card). You can then assemble all those heirloom recipes and present the bride with her own cookbook.

Invitations

Here Comes the Bride If the party is not a surprise, the bride can be a wonderful resource for your invitations. Ask her for a picture of herself and her hubby-to-be in their favorite restaurant, in their kitchen . . . any place that involves food.

1. Photocopy the couple's picture on half a piece of paper. (I can't even program my VCR, but I figured out how to do this.)

2. Fold so that the picture is on the front, and before you can say **"Emeril Lagasse,"** you have a personal invite.

Recipe of Love Compose a recipe for the couple on an index card. For instance:

Ingredients for Katie and Patrick's Life

1. Mix an endless supply of love, respect, and understanding with a pinch of spice.

2. Blend it softly with attention.

3. Whip in an overabundance of humor.

4. Freeze forever.

Add the invite info, seal, and send.

♥ **Katie and Patrick's Life** ♥

INGREDIENTS

1. love and respect and understanding
2. Spice
3. Blend
4. lots of humor
5. more humor
6. freeze forever

Leftovers Wrap a store-bought invitation in aluminum foil, as if it were leftovers. On the inside, write "Katie has enough love left over for everyone." Add party patter and off it goes.

Baby **BOTHER**

"Kitchenware Invites" I know this is not a baby shower, but go to a toy store to find inexpensive kitchenware such as:

- 🔍 **Rolling pins:** With a permanent marker, write your party patter on each pin. Wrap it in a baggie, add some confetti, then rock'n'roll!

- 🔍 **Skillet:** Photocopy and enlarge a picture of the bride (or use an original picture of the bride and groom). Cut it in a circle so that it fits in the center of a toy skillet. Use double-sided tape or glue to attach it to the center of the skillet. Write your delicious details on the back. Now you're cookin'.

Centerpieces and Creative Eye Candy

Chef's Veil Buy inexpensive paper chef's hats at your local party store. Write the bride's name on the rim and stuff with newspaper. Stand them up in the center of each table.

Homework Stand in the center of your kitchen. Gather all the objects that you use every day that can hold water: blender, coffeepot, saucepans, measuring cups, teapots. Fill them with H_2O and add flowers. Place them all in the middle of your table to create a versatile and eclectic centerpiece.

Not a Creature Was Stirring Fill a traditional vase with water. Add floral foam to the bottom. Arrange big wooden spoons, instead of flowers, in the floral foam. Allergy sufferers will applaud you.

When **Spago**, the celebrity hot spot in Beverly Hills, expanded to Orlando, the opening-night bash was far from Mickey Mouse. In the center of each guest table was a healthy and very impressive candle.

1   Buy a multiwick candle (you can find one at Pier 1).

2   Loosely tie a piece of ribbon or cord around the circumference of the candle.

3   Surround the sides with tall vegetables such as chives, asparagus, and carrots.

4   Slide the veggies under the raffia ribbon or cord and pull it tighter.

Now stand back and admire your work.

Centerpieces and Creative Eye Candy

Party Puzzle: "What's in a Name?" When two
sides of a family are merging with friends or when office mates are
meeting family, it makes for a much warmer party when there is
instant recognition of how everyone fits in. I adore creative name tags
that tell a story. For our wedding shower, buy adhesive-backed name
tags for each guest to wear. Instead of simply writing each name on the
tags, describe how the guests relate to the bride. For example:

🔍 I'm Aunt Doris, who changed Katie's first diaper.

🔍 I'm Robin . . . Katie's mother-in-law-to-be.

🔍 I'm Dee Dee, the mother of Patrick, Katie's first boyfriend.

"Who's Who?" For a spectacular name tag, photocopy a
picture of the honoree. Cut it out and glue it to an adhesive-
backed label. Personalize it for the occasion.

Baby BOTHER

🔍 For a wedding shower, add a veil.

🔍 For a baby shower, add a stomach.

🔍 For a sports party, add the appropriate ball team.

Do not shy away from creating this eye candy just because you can't
draw—most of us can't. As long as you use the photocopied picture, the
so-called artwork can be simple, satirical, and bad! It will still be great!

Place Cards

EZ Write the guest's name on a blank recipe card and place it at the appropriate place setting.

Sugar and Spice Buy inexpensive spice bottles. Write the guest's name on one, and place it at their setting.

Boy Toys Remember the kitchen toys you were thinking of buying for the invitations? Well, they have another use. Write each guest's name on a toy rolling pin or skillet with a permanent marker and use each one as a place card.

Herbaliscious Plant mini-terra-cotta pots with herbs such as sage, oregano, lavender, dill, or parsley. Write each guest's name on a planting marker, and stick it in the soil.

Big BOTHER

Apron Strings Buy inexpensive aprons at a discount store. Write each guest's name or initials on an apron with a colored marker. Tie it on the back of each partygoer's chair. If you don't want to do this for everyone, simply buy a single white apron and tie it to the back of the bride's chair.

Napkin Rings

A Girls' Best Friend In the novelty department of large party stores, I have found packages of 15 engagement rings for about $2.99. (My future husband better spend more than this.) Simply slip a rolled napkin through each ring.

Used and Abused If you haven't used the toy rolling pins or skillets yet, tie a ribbon around the handle of each skillet or each rolling pin and then tie around a napkin as a ring.

Kudos

You did a great job of throwing this wedding shower. Maybe the bride will toss you the bouquet (if you want it!).

Theme: Kidz Party

Sometimes the theme of a kidz party is dictated by your little darlin'. If you hear, "Mommy, Mommy . . . can I have a Barney party?" 3,491 times, then I would suggest skipping my little theme exercise. But if you don't want to be a merchandiser's mommy, there are other original ideas that don't require a licensing fee. I'm going to give you 10 concepts, because not all of them are little gal and little guy appropriate.

Peter's Petting Zoo

Organize an outing to your local pet store. If they have any unusual animals, learn a little something about them ahead of time, so you can pass your knowledge on to the mini-zookeepers. If you have some cash to blow, a goldfish per kid is great party loot.

Alex's Car Wash

Do a rain dance and then provide a warm sudsy pail for each child. After hosing, provide a water gun for each kid for rinsing. Look out! Bathing suits are required for the kidz, and the parents need patience.

Jimmy's Grand Slam

Look out **Mark McGwire** . . . Jimmy and his friends are taking a picnic lunch to the batting cage. And if you don't have one in your town, you can easily set up a quasi-cage in a school yard or backyard.

Becky's Beauty Parlor

Little girls today go from finger paint to face paint in a flash. Historically, young ladies have always loved to play dress up. For Becky's birthday, we'll make up all of her pint-size pals.

Treasure Hunt

I love this one . . . can't someone do this for me? It all begins with a map that each kid receives. The idea is to uncover clues as a group that will lead you to the hidden treasure.

T-Party Have each princess and her favorite doll come to this fancy luncheon. Provide the little angels with scarves, hats, and tons of accessories from your junk jewelry box. After they are dressed for the occasion, serve herbal tea and let the gals decorate tea cakes with you. This will fit them to a T.

Painter's Palace Invite each Picasso to wear old clothes and provide each of the masters with a painter's cap and gloves. Get a lot of cardboard boxes from your grocery store that each master will decorate (with very washable latex paint). They can also paint the paper tablecloth and decorate cookies for dessert.

Jewelry Jamboree Forget the salad bar . . . provide the partygoers with a jewelry bar instead, filled with all different kinds of beading supplies. You will be the recipient of many beautiful bracelet and necklace creations for years to come. You can order your beads on-line at Eclectic Etc. (www.eebeads.com).

Flower Girls Decorate each girl's face as a flower with non-toxic face paint. (It's not hard to do, and no one will judge the results.) A little color goes a long way. Provide your little flower girls with gloves, then plant seeds in individual pots that the gals can take home and nurture.

The Great Indoors

Camping in the living room? Why not! A whole night of adventure, storytelling, and bug juice is a great way to celebrate a birthday.

I'm going to go with "The Great Indoors" as my party theme

. . . because the idea of S'mores is making my mouth water!

Refreshments

If you can rustle up a couple of canteens and mess kits, it would be a great way for you to serve your hot dogs, beans, and bug juice.

- As an extra party guest, why not invite some Gummi worms into your bug juice? Using an ice cube tray, add water and one worm per cube. You don't have to cover the whole worm: a wiggling tail makes it more fun. Freeze your worm cubes. When added to your bug juice, they'll make your little guests squirm.

- I am not suggesting that you start a bonfire in your living room (especially if you don't have a fireplace), but you can toast marshmallows with graham crackers and chocolate on a kitchen hibachi or even over a gas burner.

Invitations

Enclosures You can establish an outdoor atmosphere using store-bought invitations by including some plastic bugs, leaves, or twigs in the envelope.

Mellow Out How about sending a bag of mini marshmallows to your mini campers? Simply write all of the party patter on the outside of the bag with a permanent marker.

Baby BOTHER

"Seeing the Light" Send campers flashlights with their names on them that they must bring back to gain entrance to the indoor camping site.

Centerpieces and Creative Eye Candy

The centerpiece for this "camp-in" should be the quasi-tent that you pitch in the center of the room. It can be as simple as a blanket thrown over two chairs. . . or a real tent. If kidz have their own sleeping bags, that's great. If not, pillows and blankets will work just fine.

Rover? If you have a dog, designate Spot as a coyote for the evening. If not, place stuffed animals all over the joint for a gamy atmosphere.

Men's Room Place a crooked outhouse sign, which you can make with cardboard and a crayon, over the bathroom. Remove all the bulbs from any bathroom fixtures, and use one votive candle to simulate an outdoor evening.

Storytelling Some of the creative eye candy that these kidz will see are the characters that will come to life after the lights are out. Encourage the kidz to use only their flashlights during the night . . . especially while you are reading them a scary campfire story.

The Web If you are so inclined, you can take string and drape it from an object that is taller than the kidz. Attach a fake spider to it . . . and they will be caught in a web of wonder. It goes without saying that Gummi Bears should be hidden in sleeping bags and under pillows for extra environmental thrills.

Creative Ear Candy

There are CDs and tapes that echo the sounds of a campfire or the Great Outdoors . . . even including crickets. Depending on the ages of the kidz, you may want sounds of horror and terror in the background. Try to find the CD *Bare Bones* by K. Tell. If your local store doesn't carry it, you can buy it on-line through www.amazon.com or www.cdnow.com.

Kudos

After the campers have thanked you on the way out . . . sneak into the kitchen for the leftover S'mores!

Theme: Anniversary Party

Well, well, well . . . celebrating love without the jitters of a wedding— and without the opinions of your mother-in-law. What a wonderful occasion to celebrate! So let's get going. In tackling this theme, try to bring all the personal knowledge that you have about the couple to the table. (No, I don't mean the number of times Uncle Sammy slept with Aunt Lottie.) Think more along the lines of the hobbies they share, the places they go, and the glue that holds them together.

- If they are golfers: ***Chaz and Charlie . . . Still Teeing Off After 18 Years.***

- If they are grandparents, think of the grand celebration through the perspective of the grandchildren: ***Nana and Pop Pops' Big Day.***

- If they are travelers: ***Annie and Bob . . . Still Sharing a Suitcase After 26 Years.***

- If they simply love each other, throw a ***Valentine's Day Party*** for them . . . no matter what time of year it is.

- If they are tennis players: ***Gwen and Brett's Love Match.***

Okay . . . I'm going to say "I do" to ***"Chaz and Charlie . . . Still Teeing Off After 18 Years."***

Refreshments

The Ultimate "Club" Sandwich
Rid your cupboard of all the Wonder Bread and search for the most luxurious bread you can find. (I like to use oversize Tuscan, but if you can't find that in your market, whole grain will do.) Build the club with unusual combinations.

- Apple-cured bacon, mesclun salad greens, cherry tomatoes, and smoked turkey

- Romaine lettuce, heirloom tomatoes, avocado slices, sweet onion, and tarragon grilled chicken

- Spinach leaves, sun-dried tomatoes, grilled swordfish, and mustard (with a little ginger powder mixed in)

- Baby greens, yellow tomatoes, grilled portobello mushrooms or chicken bacon

Tiger Woods Tuna Balls

No . . . this is not what they eat in the Woodses' household—and I don't even know if this champion eats tuna—but I thought that this dish had a nice ring to it. Make your favorite tuna salad recipe using white albacore tuna. Use a cracker or a small piece of bread as your base. Roll your tuna into the shape of a golf ball and press it slightly into the base. Cover your whole serving platter with lettuce greens and place your balls on your pseudo grass.

Sweet Holes in One

For $10 a box, Art Coco Chocolate (800-779-8985) makes a treat that is sure to score. These mini chocolate golf balls will make you forget your handicap (www.artcoco-chocolate.com).

Tin Cup

For one of the premiere parties for *Tin Cup,* the flick starring **Kevin Costner** and **Rene Russo**, dessert was served in a chilled—you guessed it—tin cup! You can do this for less than the price of a video rental. Choose a white ice cream or light-colored sorbet. Use an ice cream scooper to create a hole in one for dessert.

Invitations

A Little Birdie

Start with a blank piece of paper (as most authors do). Then fill it with all the golf lingo known to mankind. For instance . . .

A Little Birdie told me that Chaz and Charlie have been **on par** for 18 years. Although we are **green** with envy over their **Bogey** and Bacall relationship, we have **ironed** out our jealousy and would like **to drive** home our congratulations. Please join us in our **hole** of fun. **Follow through** by RSVPing to the starter.

Know the Score

Borrow a scorecard from your local golf course. Use a thick marker to write "After 18 years, Chaz and Charlie still know the score." Fill in the rest of the party patter and photocopy it for all of your other players.

Take Flight

Buy inexpensive or used golf balls. On each one, write "Chaz and Charlie's 18th . . . Let's have a ball!" Include the rest of your stats on a green piece of paper. Seal and send.

"Join the Club"

Baby BOTHER

Buy some toy golf clubs at your favorite discount toy store. Get out your trusty marker and invite your guests to join your "club" for the evening by writing your party patter directly on the shaft. Add a little raffia ribbon to the club . . . and off it goes.

If you're so inclined, photocopy a picture of the anniversary champions and glue it to the head of the club.

Centerpieces and Creative Eye Candy

Since Chaz and Charlie are cele-brating their 18th, it would be a winning idea to incorporate their number in a centerpiece.

- Buy some sun visors without any logos. Write the number 18 on the visor. Place the visor at the center of the table, with a small vase of short flowers in the center.

- Remember the toy golf clubs that you were thinking about getting for the invitations? Well, I hope you found them, 'cuz if you did, you can fill a tall vase with dark green lettuce leaves (pseudo grass) or sand. Instead of arranging flowers in the vase, stick in a couple of the clubs, upside down, with "18" written on each head.

Baby BOTHER

"Flag it Down" Buy some blank flags at your party store. Transform them into 18th hole flags by writing the magic number on them. Put a terra-cotta pot filled with dirt and moss in the center of each table and stick your flag into it. If you want to make your own flag, simply cut construction paper or poster board in the shape of a flag, write "18" on it, and glue it to a stick. You may want to glue a picture of the "duffers" on the back of the flag.

Big BOTHER

"Turf and Surf"

1 At Home Depot or your local nursery, pick up some Astroturf. Have them cut it in the shape of a golf green (which is good news, because it doesn't have to be even).

2 Cut a round hole anywhere on your green, so that it fits over the top of a small vase.

3 Place some piled newspapers in the center of your table to build up the height of the green so that your vase can hide underneath. (Don't worry . . . this just sounds hard.)

4 Nestle your water-filled vase and cover it with your green.

5 Make sure that the hole is over the top of your vase.

6 Add flowers to your vase—and admire. It is so cute that it almost makes me want to take up the game!

Creative Eye Candy

Place Cards

Have a Ball Write each person's name on a used golf ball and tee it off at their place setting.

Forget Me Not! Hang a visor off each guest's chair with his or her name on it. This eye candy is especially enlightening, 'cuz you won't forget a name when your guests wear them.

Napkin Rings

The Good Ol' Days On an anniversary, it's always a hoot to remember days gone by. Photocopy a picture of Chaz and Charlie from their wedding day. Cut it to about 2 inches by 2 inches. Scotch-tape the picture to the center of a foot-long piece of green ribbon or raffia. Now tie the ribbon around an old oak tree . . . sorry, I meant to say a napkin.

Kudos   Yell "Fore," and Take a Bow.

Theme: Oscar Party

The Big Kahuna, the night of nights . . . Several hundred million of us worldwide tune in each year to watch cut-off acceptance speeches and to see who is wearing what. Some of us like to watch the festivities alone, under the covers, eating raisin bran. But if you want to share the night, let's get started by dressing up our theme exercise.

Jimmy the Greek
Send out a ballot to the guests ahead of time, giving the odds on each nominee. Include some Monopoly money (since I'm sure you don't have a gaming license) for them "to bet" on the winners.

Dress-up Party Have each guest arrive in over-the-top Oscar garb.

The Golden Age Have each guest come as a notable past winner or loser.

Oscar 20?? Plan the evening around this year's nominated films.

Film Buffs Party in the nude . . . just kidding! Invite a local drama teacher, film historian, or a cinema know-it-all, to add Oscar color throughout the evening.

And the Oscar goes to . . .

I'm going to go with **"Dress-up Party,"** 'cuz if I'm all pushed up and tucked in, why shouldn't you be?

I've been covering the world's most glamorous event for more than 12 years. Each year, I get dolled up in a very expensive, magnificent gown (which I borrow), by designer extraordinaire Pilar Rossi. I wear over $1 million worth of dazzling Harry Winston jewels (which I also borrow). And half the night I wear sneakers (which I own) to climb up to a 100-foot platform, where I am held captive for over nine hours to broadcast. What a glamorous life!

Refreshments

Traditionally, the menu for the Governor's Ball, which is the party that the Oscar participants attend, is planned months in advance by superchef Wolfgang Puck and the ball's committee. Seventeen hundred starving stars and producers cannot wait to chow down after such a long, exhausting show. Recent offerings include star-shaped smoked salmon and caviar, medallions of veal, white Alaskan salmon, orange-ginger stir-fry and chocolate Oscars with gold dust for dessert.

But I think you should have fun with the food at your party; incorporate movies past and present into it. These dishes may sound silly, but they'll win the prize on Oscar night.

- *Godfather* Pasta Primavera
- *As Good as It Gets* Spinach
- *Little Mermaid* Halibut
- *Shakespeare in Love* Fish and Chips
- Bette Davis Rib "Eyed" Steaks
- Tom Hanks Hash
- *Saving Private O'Ryan* Potatoes
- *Forrest Gump* Chocolates

Invitations

Star Gazing If you would like to go the store-bought route and can't find anything appropriate, just take a blank piece of paper, add some star decals, and tell your guests, "Instead of coming as you are, come as a star!"

The Envelope, Please Take an envelope and write "The Envelope, Please" on the outside. Slip the party particulars inside and send this duo as an envelope within an envelope.

"Props, Please" Buy any symbol of the Academy Awards: sunglasses, hair spray, film, etc. Add your party patter, and you're the winner! Send your invite in a bag or envelope decorated with star decals.

Baby BOTHER

"Seeing Red" Go to your local carpet-remnant store and beg for scraps of red carpet. Cut the carpet into small pieces, about two inches by two inches, with a heavy-duty scissors. Stuff your carpet and some red tissue paper into an envelope, and invite your guests to walk down the red carpet on Oscar night . . . dressed as a star.

Centerpieces and Creative Eye Candy

Here's a reminder for all of your nominees: always return to the think tank to help you come up with a centerpiece idea.

Think *conversation piece*

Think *humor*

Think *grand and glorious*

Think *earthy and edible*

Conversation piece and humor seem to be the categories that would fit this type of occasion.

Popcorn Container Save an oversize plastic-coated popcorn container from your last visit to the candy counter. Wash it, then place a small vase with cut flowers inside.

Big Basket Fill a basket or a bowl with movie candies, such as Raisinets, Sno-Caps, Goobers, Twizzlers, Junior Mints.

Or you can focus on Hollywood's box-office giants, past and present. Since I'm not Kreskin, I don't know what this year's biggest movies will be . . . so we'll just have to live in the past here.

Forrest Gump Pile up boxes of chocolates to remind your guests that "life is like a box of chocolates."

The English Patient Place a vase filled with English roses in a kid's doctor bag. (Any kind of roses will do, just say that they're English—it's called acting).

Philadelphia Fill a big barrel with fat Philly pretzels flanked by mustard.

Jurassic Park Raid your kid's toy chest and borrow a dinosaur . . . or buy a couple (of different sizes) at the toy store. This centerpiece will never become extinct.

The Postman Place a canvas bag overflowing with letters in the center of the table.

Let's just say I'm glad *Arachnophobia* was never up for best picture!!

Creative Eye Candy

Place Cards

"You Oughta Be in Pictures" As each of your star invitees enter, they are, of course, met by the annoying paparazzo (who happens to be your uncle Herbie with a Polaroid). Take each Polaroid picture and place it at the appropriate place setting.

Napkin Rings: "Candy Is Dandy" Carefully slip the wrappers off some candy bars that you would buy at the movies, and hide the candy so you won't eat it! Place your napkin inside the wrapper for a cozy silver-screen napkin ring.

Corny Sew together about 6 inches of popcorn on a string. Tie the two ends together to make a ring. Then simply slip your napkin into your popcorn ring . . . and don't add any butter or salt!

Kudos

The ballots are counted, and you have won your category. Prepare your acceptance speech.

Theme: All-Grown-Up * Birthday Parties *

When I was younger, I looked forward to my date of birth because I adored the gooey, rich birthday cake. Not that my teen years are antiques, I no longer allow myself to indulge in buttercream and find that each year it's getting harder and harder to blow out all of the birthday candles. Okay . . . that's a big stretch . . . but I am trying to make a point here. Birthday parties are tricky. Not everyone wants to acknowledge passing decades publicly. So before you go out and buy the candles, make sure that your celebrant wants to celebrate. Once you get the green light . . . let's rev the engine.

Adult birthday bashes should be customized, personalized—no generic brands. Do your theme exercises, and focus on the passions of your victim or his or her magic number. Perhaps one of the following suggestions will hit the spot.

Josh's Speedway Toward 30:
Josh is obsessed with cars. We're going to celebrate the fact that his own model (the Josh, made in 1971) is well oiled and needs no spare parts at 30.

Dana's Pampering Party
Aunt Dana is selfless and never takes time out for herself. We're gonna change all that, even if it's just for an afternoon. Guests will be encouraged to bring gifts that are nurturing and pampering. A local hairdresser will come to the house to give her a makeover, and everyone will wait on her, hand and foot (especially since her feet now have painted toenails).

Annie's Miss America Party

Annie is turning 50, and she's not too thrilled about that number. Her mom remembered that Annie's high school dream was to become Miss America (yeah, I'm not kidding), so she is throwing her daughter a tongue-in-cheek Miss America surprise party.

80 Years Young

Nana is 80, so we're gonna showcase each decade with the history and highlights of her life. Partygoers representing each decade will write in a memory journal—complete with pictures—as a tribute to Nana. It could be as simple as photocopied pages stapled together or as complex as a bound book.

The Ninth Anniversary of Steven's 39th

Since my pal Steven now has one or two gray hairs, he likes to mark the passing years in a kinder, gentler way. The theme may become a tad repetitive, but each year, something new is brought to the table. The gifts always revolve around Steven's obsession with youth (which gets funnier with each passing year).

But no matter how young Steven stays, he can never be Miss America—and that's the theme we're going to crown.

Refreshments

Out of respect for the bathing suit competition, a delicious, low-fat menu should be served.

"Bikini Blintzes" filled with cottage cheese instead of sour cream.

"Silicon Salad" implanted with nonfat vinaigrette.

"Spike-Heel Sangria" spiked with diet cranberry juice and fresh fruit.

"One-piece Pizza" made with pita bread and skim mozzarella (no pun intended).

"Runway Raspberry Sorbet" served on nonfat angel food cake.

"Atlantic City's Favorite Salt Water Taffy"—sorry, they don't make it nonfat.

Invitations

Petal Pusher If you want to go the "store-bought" route, try to find something with flowers on it. Then place some dried rose petals in the envelope for that Miss America touch.

Banner Day Write the guest's name vertically on a long strip of satin ribbon, as if it were a contestant's sash. Then write all your party particulars on the rest of the fabric, and you have a wearable invite.

Baby BOTHER

Crowning Glory

🔍 Find something in a party store that could represent Annie's Crowning Glory, and attach all the party particulars.

🔍 Photocopy a picture of Annie's face. Draw a crown on top of her head with a gold pen. (Don't make a face, it's easy: just draw three upside-down triangles.) Use the reverse side to fill in the dreamy details (time, date, place, etc.). Then invite your fellow contestants to Annie's Miss America soiree.

Centerpieces and Creative Eye Candy

Royal Blush
Since you probably don't have any crowns lying around in your closet, try to find some in a novelty shop or party supply store. Place each one in the center of your table, wrapped around a vase filled with flowers.

Stuff It
Stuff a bikini top with tissues, then tie it around the widest part of your vase. Fill your vase with blooming beauties.

Baby BOTHER

"Shoe Fetish" Search for some old high heels in thrift shops. Fill each with damp floral sponge and press short flowers into the sponge until the vamp of the shoe is entirely covered.

Napkin Rings

"Flower Power" Tie a 12-inch piece of ribbon around the center of a flower stalk. Roll the napkin and tie the ribboned flower around it.

Baby BOTHER

"Va-va-va-voom!"

- Cut out a small picture of Annie's head.
- Find a va-va-va-voom picture of a bikini-clad model.
- Glue Annie's head over the model's for an instant body fit.
- Photocopy this picture of the new-and-maybe-not-so-improved Annie. Scotch-tape the center of an 8-inch piece of ribbon to the back of the picture, and you have a napkin ring.

Place Cards

"Please Be Seated" Remember the sash that you were going to make for each contestant as an invitation? Well, if you didn't go that route, you can use the same idea to make a winning place card. Simply write each contestant's name vertically on a long piece of satin ribbon, and attach it to the back of the appropriate chair.

Annie's Throne

It would be so gauche for our little Miss America to sit in the same sort of seat as her ladies-in-waiting. Decorate a large chair with any ostentatious robe, tablecloth, or bedspread that you have around the house. Add some cushy soft pillows, and you've just thrown together a throne.

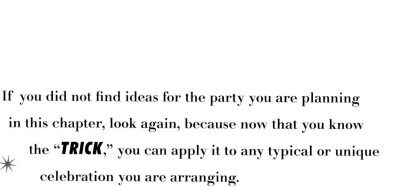

Kudos

Here she comes . . .
Miss Party Giver!

Party Pooped

If you did not find ideas for the party you are planning in this chapter, look again, because now that you know the "**TRICK**," you can apply it to any typical or unique celebration you are arranging.

Peggy Siegal, of Lizzie Grubman PR, The Peggy Siegal Company, is an East Coast hostess with the mostest. She has planned hundreds of smashing events for the entertainment industry, and believes that you should give a lot of thought to your guest list. The right mix of people should be a primary element of your party planning. And remember that you *don't* have to limit your list to folks that have a lot in common. Fantastic conversations are sometimes born out of differences!

One Size Fits All

Some fantastic party ideas are universal (except maybe the pink rum punch served in baby bottles); they can be modified for most situations. With a little nip and tuck here and there (no Hollywood pun intended), you can use these bountiful brainstorms for your bash.

When actress **Lela Rochon** tied the knot at her dream wedding to director Antoine Fugue, the 320 guests were given silver- and gold-plated bells. After the ceremony, when the newlyweds walked back down the aisle, the guests rang the bells en masse. Whether you're planning a wedding for hundreds or a birthday dinner for 17, it's energizing to have the celebrants do something together. In keeping with togetherness, the hostess at an Italian feast I once attended handed out the words to *La Traviata* to all of her guests. They were written phonetically so none of us were intimidated. After we polished off the pasta, the music was blaring, and we all stood up and sang for our supper. It was magnifico.

Picture Place Mat

Kinko's will laminate a place mat picture montage of your friends and family for $5.99. It is washable and can be used over and over again. I've used baby pictures for a 65th-birthday party and pictures of absent relatives that live far away for Thanksgiving. I've even used pictures of old boyfriends for a wedding shower—you can drip on those!

You've Been Framed

Whenever I see small picture frames on sale, I snatch them up. Create a unique seating plan by putting a picture of your guest in a frame at his or her place setting. It's a great take-home gift.

You can also use framed pictures as napkin rings. Scotch-tape ribbon to the back of the frame and tie the ribbon around the napkin! I used these napkin rings at a "Work of Art" party that was held at a museum. Framing a younger picture of the beautiful celebrant is always fun.

At a recent official Oscar bash, each guest received an antique picture frame that contained the evening's menu done in calligraphy. The celebrities got to take this memento home with them. (Quite frankly, I would have rather taken home a picture of **Tom Hanks**.)

Kibbles & Bits Napkin Rings

I realize that not everyone has birthday parties for their dogs, but when my Shih Tsu reached the milestone of 21 (in dog years, of course), we celebrated! I didn't serve Alpo in the shape of a 21, but I did use Milk-Bone dog biscuits as napkin rings.

No matter what the occasion, ribbon can make almost any object into a napkin ring. Just tie some ribbon around . . .

- Shells for a seafood dinner
- Keys for a housewarming party
- Lollipops for a kids' party
- Live flowers . . . for any occasion

Licorice can also be used as a delicious ribbon. Simply tie it in a bow around a napkin . . . for kids 1 to 100!

Vases

Sorry, Mr. Steuben, but glass vases can be boring. At the premiere of the film *Backdraft,* the florist used a fire pail as a vase for each table. For the opening of the Broadway show *High Society,* the flowers were housed inside upside-down top hats. At a studio party for *Saving Private Ryan,* the floral arrangements seemed to grow out of army pith helmets.

Baby BOTHER

Tutti Frutti

For any occasion, fruits and vegetables are not only healthy for you but also make wonderful vases. For mini arrangements, I like to use oranges, squashes, eggplants, melons, and gourds.

1. **Cut the fruit or vegetable in half.**
2. **Scoop out the guts.**
3. **Place a little wet floral Styrofoam in the bottom of the fruit or veggie.**
4. **Cut your flowers so that they are proportionate to your fruit or veggie.**
5. **Push the stems into the Styrofoam and there you have it!**

Any container that has personality can be turned into a vase. If you just look around your home, you'll probably find:

🔍 **Teapots**

🔍 **Tennis ball cans**

🔍 **Beach pails**

🔍 **Watering cans**

But if you still want to use a vase from Steuben or Target, please fill it creatively.

"XOXOXOXO" For this huggable arrangement, you'll need two vases: one inexpensive bubble vase that you can buy anywhere and a smaller cylinder vase. This effect is so versatile and magical. I use it all the time!

1 Fill the small cylinder vase with water and flowers, and place it in the center of your larger vase.

2 Fill the remainder of the big vase with candy kisses; be sure to surround the little vase to its top rim. It should look as if the flowers are floating in a sea of candy. . . . Sweet and sensational.

You can replace the candy with one of the following to create this floating effect:

🔍 **Lemons and limes**

🔍 **Blueberries**

🔍 **Trail mix**

🔍 **Dried oranges**

- ● **Shells**
- ● **Gummi Bears**
- ● **Nuts**
- ● **Lollipops**
- ● **Mini pumpkins**
- ● **Autumn leaves**
- ● **M&M's**
- ● **Multicolored peppers**
- ● **Coffee beans**

"Something's Fishy" Yes, I'm not kidding . . . a couple of goldfish swimming around your flowers can create a golden moment. You have to try this one—and don't forget to feed them!

And if **Kevin Costner** floats your boat . . . here's a little somethin' he likes to do. Take a large shell and fill it with water. Then add floating votive candles or floating gardenias. (You can always use a big bowl, if shells are scarce.)

Cover-ups I don't eat red meat anymore, but I find butcher paper irresistible. Sometimes I wrap presents in it and tie with plain string—but that's a whole other chapter!

For kids' parties, I like to crisscross two long pieces of butcher paper across the table. Using acrylic paint or colorful Magic Markers, you can draw on this paper tablecloth, write the guests' names on it, or let the kids doodle on it.

If you are brave, you can provide finger paints for the party guests, and create a work of art out of the tablecloth.

Rugs, Shawls, Scarves, and Quilts
These interesting alternatives to tablecloths usually won't cover the whole table, but you can drape them and set them at unusual angles. That's part of the charm.

Plastic Transparent Tablecloths
Whatever you choose to display—magazines, newspapers, pictures, pressed flowers—can be protected by laminate cover.

Place Cards
Not every place card needs to be a big bother. Just take your friendly laundry marker (or my new favorite—fabric pens), and write your guests' names on:

- **Leaves**
- **Vegetables**
  (such as mini pumpkins)
- **Candy**

- **Twigs**
- **Stones**
- **Golf balls**
- **Ribbons**

The Guest of Honor

Let's face it . . . it's always an "honor" to be seated next to the celebrant, but you know that's not always possible—unless you use this old trick.

Baby **BOTHER**

- Photocopy a picture of the party animal.

- Have the photocopies enlarged so that they are nearly life-size. (You may have to use several pieces of paper . . . Kinko's can probably do it cheaply.)

- Glue your enlarged prints to a large piece of poster board.

- Cut out your new "clones" and place them in a seat of honor at every table. Aren't you glad your mother taught you to share?

Everything's Coming Up Roses

Baby **BOTHER**

For envelope flower-power, send all of your invites with floral stamps that you can buy at any post office. Use a daughter's green felt marker to extend the stem down the side of the envelope. It doesn't matter if you're not an artist . . . you don't even have to draw a straight line!

Mr. Marc Balinsky
444 East 82nd Street
Apartment Two R
New York, New York
1 . 0 . 0 . 2 . 8

Candle Power

Candles are not just for romance. You save on electricity, offer flattering light, and proclaim a special environment when you use them. Place votives in unexpected places: going up staircases . . . in bathrooms . . . on top of refrigerators . . .

in fireplaces. And if you want to play dress-up with votives, place them in cored apples, oranges, or lemons.

Bored Game?

If you are simply bored with flowers and candles on your table, try to match the centerpiece to the food you are serving.

Chinese Food Ask your local restaurant for some extra unused containers. Place tall, dripless candles inside the containers. Surround them with Chinese noodles for extra whimsy. You can also put short glasses inside the containers and fill them with some short flowers. I found an "oversize" Chinese food container in a party store and often fill it with bountiful fruit for any occasion.

Seafood Take a fish bowl and fill it with goldfish. Fill a beach pail with flowers. Accessorize it with sand shovels.

Brunch Use ceramic teapots of different sizes as vases. You don't need to borrow Grandma's—you can buy them at most department stores.

- Fill a tall electric coffeepot with breadsticks.
- Empty coffee cans and fill them with flowers, dried fruits, or candies.
- Place a silver tray (which you can get at any flea market) in the center of the table and fill it with jams, jellies, and cut flowers.

Italian Food I did "the ol' wine bottle extravaganza" in college, but it still holds up 99 years later! Use empty assorted-size Italian wine bottles as candleholders. To make the candle fit, melt the bottom of it over heat until it becomes pliable. Every local pizzeria has a Chianti bottle on each table, but when you use a half-dozen different ones, it makes quite a statement! (Don't worry—the statement is not that you've been drinking all afternoon to empty the bottles!)

Breadbasket Forget about serving Wonder Bread with dinner . . . Instead, be creative with hearty breads and stay within your budget. Simply line your breadbasket or a bowl with a fabric napkin, then over-stuff with different types and sizes of bread. If you throw in some whole walnuts and a nutcracker, you will have created a centerpiece that your guests will go nuts for (sorry, I hope that joke gets edited out!).

The Eyes Wide Shut Gala

This sophisticated and magical evening honoring **Tom Cruise** and **Nicole Kidman** actually took place in the parking lot of Chasen's, a legendary Beverly Hills restaurant. Because the film was sensual in nature, party planner extraordinaire Mary Micucci made sure that sultry music danced through the air. Always remember to set the mood with music and make sure the volume is appropriate for your crowd. Since you'll be so busy (you little party animal), why don't you put someone else in charge of the music?

My Beautiful Balloon

This is a swell invite for many occasions. Put a piece of paper that has all of your party patter on it in a balloon, blow it up, and tie a knot. Deliver in person if your guests live close by. If not . . . send it flat in an envelope!

You're Invited!
Sam's Birthday
April 20th, 8pm
RSVP 555-1234

Cheap Treats

Yes, you sometimes have to buy in bulk . . . but Oriental Trading Company in Quebec, Canada (888-353-9850) has novelties galore for prices you can't ignore. I bought mini chalkboards for 50 cents each that I use for invitations and menus at dinner parties; checkers sets and mini basketball sets for 40 cents each that I put in grab bags for some of my younger guests, and fantastic 16-inch beach balls that I recently used in lieu of rice at a oceanside wedding on Cape Cod that set me back only $3.99 for the entire bulk! Their merchandise is constantly changing, so call for their catalog or visit their Website at www.oriental.com.

Be on the Lookout

I'm not talking about big-ticket items, but every once in a while, buy what ya don't need. If there's a little extra $ in the piggy bank, and a prop catches your eye . . . whip out that wallet. I once bought a lot of "chair" paraphernalia for absolutely no reason . . . until one of my friends became "Chairman of the Board." What a party it was!

"Personal Pot"

Baby BOTHER

No . . . it's not illegal . . . I promise. I did this for my mother-in-law's 70th-birthday party (she looks forty). But "it" can be nipped and tucked for many occasions.

| **Photocopy many different pictures of your victim in black and white.**

2. Glue them onto a terra-cotta pot, overlapping some of the edges.

3. Shellac the pictures for an antique look . . . or just leave them alone.

4. Add a mini ficus tree with some sunflowers nestled in the leaves. You've created a centerpiece that can forever be enjoyed as a personal pot.

The Party's Over

As you're accepting your standing ovation for throwing such a super soiree, I don't want you to collapse from exhaustion. Remember, *you* are also a guest at your party. Don't just work it—the real **"TRICK"** is to enjoy it. Please "bother" to do as much preparation ahead of time, so you too can enjoy the memorable moments. If it all seems overwhelming for you, take it down a few notches in the planning stages . . . don't plan more than you can handle. A few touches go a long way.

The party's over for now . . . but your party-planning **"TRICK**ery" has just begun!

It's a Wrap

We've all been taught not to judge a book by its cover, but sometimes we just can't help it. Not that I'm judging his cover, but **Leonardo DiCaprio** gave certain members of the cast and crew of The Beach little trinkets wrapped in shells! During the filming of Gone With the Wind, **Clark Gable** gave **Vivien Leigh** a necklace for her birthday, wrapped in fabric from one of her final costumes. I know your wrapping materials may be "gone with the wind"—with some leftover Christmas wrapping and about 4 inches of frayed ribbon stuffed in the back of a drawer—but I have good news! You don't need it. This chapter is chock-full of alternative ideas to ye ol' traditional wrap, and after you read it, you'll be able to handle any wrapping emergencies. In some cases even the gift will become secondary!

What, No Wrapping Paper?

It's never around when we need it, but have no fear. Great creative substitutes surround you. You may never have to go to the stationery store again!

| The newspaper. Use a section of the paper that corresponds to the interests of your gift recipient as a wrap.

- **Stock quotes** (with some folded-dollar-bill flourishes)
- **Sports**
- **Home**
- **Comics** (with a lollipop bonus!)
- **Travel**
- **Business**
- **Beauty** (with lipstick under the ribbon)
- **Food**
- **TV listings**
- **Classifieds**

2 Ye ol' brown paper bag. Empty your groceries and wrap away.

3 **Plastic garbage bags** (unused, of course). Twist the top and tie with a ribbon.

4 **Pillow cases.**

5 **Transparent plastic wrap** from the cleaners. Don't use this wrap for kids' gifts, as it can be dangerous.

Smooth as Silk Once, when I was really desperate, I made a gift bundle out of my favorite silk scarf, with the understanding that I would get it back. Now I use this technique on a regular basis. Sometimes I even use a ribbon instead of a scarf. The Silk Trading Company in L.A. (323-954-9280) specializes in tailored and sumptuous silk draperies. They sell their fabric in small quantities. Silk Trading has a catalog and will ship their merchandise anywhere.

Baby BOTHER **For Weddings, Engagements, Sweet 16s ... Including Cash Gifts**

Ask your local fabric store to cut big squares of inexpensive tulle. I prefer white, but it comes in assorted colors.

1 Place the present in the center of the fabric square.

2 Pull up all four corners.

3 Twist and tie with a ribbon.

4 You can use multicolor layers (three or four fabric pieces) for a magical look.

And while you're in the fabric store, rummage through the inexpensive remnant area for interesting fabric squares, which make a great wrapping-paper alternative for liquor or wine.

1 **Place the bottle or box in the center of the fabric square.**

2 **Pull up all four corners.**

3 **Twist, tie, and cheers!**

When a bigwig studio gift consultant needs fabulous fabrics for wrapping, he jets all the way from the left coast to the right, to Joe's Fabrics Warehouse on the Lower East Side of Manhattan. It's a large discount warehouse with eclectic and elegant fabrics. There are so many fabrics that it's impossible to see them all in a day. But that's where Mimi, the perfect proprietress, comes in . . . she's a shortcut to creativity. When I needed yellow fabric with teddy bears on it for one of my projects, I simply called the marvelous Mimi, and it was in the mail the next day. You should place her number (212-674-7089) in the permanent section of your Rolodex.

 **You Ought to Be in Pictures!**

Get a photograph that applies to the occasion:

- **Couple (for an anniversary or wedding)**

- **Baby picture (for birthdays from 1 to 99)**

- **Dad (for Father's Day, birthday, etc.)**

Next, copy the photo in color or black and white. Be sure to make enough copies so that your photo wrapping paper will fit the size of your present. If you're lucky, your local copy joint can Xerox multiple pages on oversize paper. If necessary, Scotch-tape the photo pages together, and start wrappin'. It's worth it.

OR (if you're computer savvy) . . .

If you feel like "bothering" a bit more, you can even scan your photograph (or photographs) into your computer, and save it on a disk. Once you've done that, you can take your disk to Kinko's and let them do the rest! They will multiply your images and print them onto **ACTUAL WRAPPING PAPER!** to give your gift the perfect personal touch. This idea is so great that it doesn't even matter what you're wrapping!

911 Emergency! Help!! No Scotch Tape?!

I know that sinking feeling when you go to the drawer and find there's only 1 inch of tape left on the dispenser. Have no fear . . . nail polish is here. That's right. In an emergency, nail polish will hold two paper surfaces together. After applying it, press the edges together for about 30 seconds . . . you've nailed it!

Snookie's Chocolate Chip Cookies
The treat of the moment in Hollywood, these cookies are delivered locally, in cellophane bundles, but this company also bothers to deliver ice-cold milk in a bucket to cookie lovers (800-927-3747). Buckets (plastic or metal) are great objects to store in your basement to wrap those unusual items. Remember, "wrap" doesn't always have to mean wrapping paper.

✳ *Boxing*

✳ No, I am not going to wrap Muhammad Ali . . .
we're going to talk about boxes, and what
to do when you don't have one.

As storage space becomes more limited in our lives, it's hard to find that nook and cranny for all of your clumsy boxes . . . so buy flat ones. Most large national chain stores sell them. Always use what you have. If you are looking for a jewelry box for earrings, and all you have is the box your vase came in . . . use it anyway! Stuff it with tissue paper, newspaper, candy, leaves, potpourri, or even a silk scarf (which I hope you'll get back).

Once, when I was strolling on the left bank of the Seine, I saw **Madonna** come out of the most charming lingerie boutique weighed down with many beautifully wrapped packages. Many dollars later, I too had one of these unusually wrapped treasures. For years, I've tried to re-create the woven envelopes, and recently I found this woven box for $5.94 at Pier 1: Ooh la la.

Naked Boxes Oops! Who

decided that we have to cover boxes with wrapping paper? The guy who owns the wrapping paper store? A lot of times naked is good . . . as long as the lights are off. Anyway, bare boxes have loads of potential.

"Kidz Presents" Have Johnny finger paint, crayon, or stick decals all over the box.

"XOXOXO" Okay . . . let's vamp. Put on the reddest lipstick you own, make sure no one is watching you, and start to kiss the box repeatedly, transferring your lip print to the gift. This method isn't just for Valentine's Day: kisses are welcome any day.

"Sealed with a Kiss" Kathy Bransfield is a wonderful whimsical jewelry designer (she has a catalog) in Santa Monica, California (310-582-1596). When wrapping her treasures for her clients, she always uses a plain box and puts one Hershey's kiss inside.

"Name Game" If you have a laundry marker and can write, you're in business. On the box, write the name of the person that the gift is going to, on an angle, multiple times, until the top surface of the box is covered. Now you have an instant one-of-a-kind presentation.

"$ and Scents" Here's an aromatic way to give a gift. Take a cotton ball and dab the inside of the box with perfume or scented oil. Don't use cologne or toilet water, because the scent won't last.

Baby BOTHER **Stampede** I am lovin' this one. You can find an amazing variety of stamps and inkpads to truly fit any occasion. An extensive stamp Website that has everything under the sun is www.rubberd.com (they are located in Rockville, Maryland, call 301-570-8853). When I was wrapping a gift for triplets, I found a stamp of three little babies holding hands . . . too cute! So apply some ingenuity to your naked box.

Place your stamp on the inkpad and then stamp away . . . all over the surface of the box. Inkpads also come in muchos color choices. I especially like antique gold, because it makes the stamp look hand-painted.

Baby BOTHER ## Personalized Tissue Paper If you know who Ringo Starr is, you'll remember when tissue paper only came in white. Now, Ringo's hair is starting to turn white, and tissue paper is available in a kaleidoscope of colors and patterns. It's also easy to personalize it to fit any occasion, especially with those terrific inkpads and stamps. Since stamps are now offered to fit any situation, I always keep a number of them on hand. My present repertoire includes a German shepherd, a piñata, a lobster, and a stiletto-heeled shoe.

Just open the inkpad and stamp the tissue paper every 2 inches or so with your desired image. Kate's Paperie (800-809-9880) carries incredible double-initial stamps that come in every letter combination imaginable. It's $5 for both the first- and last-name initials. You now have a "Why Bother? Why Not!" stamp of approval.

Stamp Co., a company based in Ventura, California, will customize any letter combo you need. They are quick, inexpensive, and reliable (805-648-4410 or www.stampco.com).

"You Gotta Have Heart" After the CEO of a large production company had triple-bypass surgery, the studio became a big benefactor of the American Heart Foundation. At holiday time, they donated to the foundation in corporate names. They sent out notification of these donations by wrapping them in red velvet heart-shaped boxes. A good idea for a good cause.

Please Leave a Message

Most art-supply stores carry press-on letters that don't require glue or Scotch tape. With these letters, you can form initials or monograms or even spell out a message on the outside of your box. They are now available in a multitude of fonts, from sophisticated to silly.

Put the Top Down!

Valerie's (310-274-7348), the quintessential makeup emporium in the heart of Beverly Hills, services the faces of **Halle Berry**, **Britney Spears**, **Wynonna Judd**, and **Goldie Hawn** to name a few. When Valerie delivers to her VIP clients, she takes the top off the box and then fills it with a small vase that holds an aromatic gardenia floating in water. The makeup is fitted between the vase and the box. This presentation is enough to get me to wear makeup on Sundays . . . my skin's day off. You too can leave the top down and surround your gift with goodies.

"A Flower Box" This is worth the effort on a small box, but it's a pain in the neck on a big one. Glue dried flowers to the entire surface of the top of the box. The presentation is really lovely, so it becomes two gifts in one! For an easier version, cover Styrofoam initials (which you can buy in chain stores or craft shops) with moss. Add a couple of real or silk flowers and you're in business! (The dragonfly is optional!)

When **Susan Sarandon** and **Tim Robbins** were staying at the Four Seasons Hotel in Beverly Hills for the Oscars, an eight-tiered hatbox tower was delivered to them from their studio. It stood about 5 feet high, with a tower formed by hatboxes of different sizes. It could have been filled with rubies and sapphires (I never did find out), but Gummi Bears would have worked just fine, since the presentation was so fantastic.

This technique is not reserved for Academy Award winners. All you need is an idea, assorted boxes, and three long pieces of ribbon.

Big BOTHER

If you want to get fancy, you can find heart-shaped boxes, crescent-shaped boxes, or hatboxes at most upscale craft stores or fancy paper stores, such as Kate's Paperie in Manhattan's SoHo (800-809-9880). This idea also works wonderfully with rectangular boxes that you can buy at national chain stores.

Now for the idea . . . think "personal" and "custom." Begin by placing tissue inside each box along with the items of your choice. Some of the towers I've built include:

Romance A split of champagne, a Sinatra CD, bubble bath, and a baby-sitter's phone number.

Teenage Girl A different color of Hard Candy nail polish in each box. You can also do this with lipsticks, hair ornaments, paperbacks, teen magazines, and CDs.

Italian Chef A new pasta cookbook, two red-and-white-checked napkins, a timer, designer tomato sauce, a wooden spoon, and pasta tongs.

Golf Tees, balls, a new golf glove, a visor, and sunblock.

Bon Voyage A disposable camera, travel alarm clock, a plastic deflatable airplane pillow, a great paperback, Dramamine, and prestamped envelopes.

You don't need to spend a lot of money or mortgage your house to pay for the contents of this tower. Fill the boxes with

- *Assorted candies*
- *Nuts*
- *Spices*
- *Herbs*
- *Chocolates*
- *Paper clips, thumbtacks, rubber bands*

- *Potpourri*
- *Photographs*
- *IOU certificates*
  (for baby-sitting, washing windows, a free Sunday afternoon, housecleaning)

You now have a tower of power!

911 Emergency! What? No Box?! Maybe you

don't need one . . .

The Old Cracker Jack Routine Also known as putting a "treat" inside
of another "treat."

- **Cash** inside a **monopoly game**

- **Airline tickets** inside a **travel book**

- A **spa gift certificate** inside a **jar of bath salts**

- **Tennis tournament tickets** inside a **can of balls**

- **Rock concert tix** inside the group's **CD case**

- **Baseball tickets** inside a **baseball cap**

- A gift I received from my love . . . a **brand-new
  camera** inside an **antique camera** (which you
  can find at a flea market for under $5)

- A gift certificate for weeding, **gardening**, plants,
  or flowers inside a **terra-cotta pot**

One year, my beau gave me cold, hard cash in an ingenious way: he
found a turn-of-the-century "dough" machine and
placed the bills inside. Don't you just love him?!

    This method also works wonders when you
have to wrap the impossible. For instance . . .

- **A puppy:** put a leash and the dog's papers
  inside a box of dog bones.

- 🔍 **A car** (lucky you): put the title inside a car magazine.

- 🔍 **A couch:** put a picture of the new one inside a pillow of the old one.

Bundles of Joy No, I'm not going to teach you how to wrap a newborn, but this technique does work well with odd shapes and items that are not in boxes. Cut a large square or rectangle out of tissue paper, cellophane, fabric, or wrapping paper. Place the gift in the center. Raise all four corners together. Twist and secure with ribbon, cord, or even a rubber band. If you want to get fancy, you can fan out the top tail.

Props I love to wrap items in unusual containers. I tend to buy in bulk when I find that special something. For a while, it was Chinese food containers, then it was terra-cotta planters. Now my wrap du jour is mini supermarket shopping carts that I bought at Cost Plus in L.A. for $4.98 each. I simply stick the item in the cart, add a little tissue paper and a ribbon, and I hit bonus-coupon day!

The Ultimate Bag Lady
Remember how we name-dropped on the naked box? Well, we're gonna do it on a bag.

1 Take out your colored markers.

2 Flatten the bag.

3 Write the name of the recipient of the gift on an angle, multiple times.

4 Repeat on the back side of the bag.

5 Stick the present inside your personalized shopping bag.

6 Tie the handles of the bag together with long strands of ribbon to finish it off.

You can also use a brown grocery bag without handles.

Baby Face
Enlarge a baby picture of your gift recipient using a copy machine. Glue or Scotch-tape the picture to both sides of the bag. You can adjust your treatment to match your occasion. For instance:

- For a going-away gift, add a flag of Italy (if they are going to Italy, of course)

- For a "get well" bag, add pictures of aspirin or members of the cast of ER

- For an anniversary present, add a wedding picture

- For a back-to-school bonus, add book covers

- For a tooth-fairy bag, add ☺ smiles ☺

Finishing Touches

After a present is signed, sealed, and about to be delivered, it's not ready to go without those final special touches. I think of them as dessert. A cake can be extraordinarily scrumptious, but without some icing . . . it's still not finished. So get ready to smear it on.

Awesome Accents

After you have completed fussing with your masterpiece, slip a few pieces of the following under your ribbon, bow, or knot:

- **Sprigs of lavender**
- **Rosemary or thyme**
- **Dried flowers**
- **Silk flowers**
- **Live flowers**
- **Leaves**
- **Twigs**
- **Mistletoe**
- **Instant chicken soup** (for flu sufferers)

On page 45, I told you about three fantastic gift bags to present to someone who's been your lifesaver. Here are other ways to wrap with accents, depending on the occasion.

- 🔍 **A cigar**
- 🔍 **A pacifier**
- 🔍 **A candy or granola bar**

- 🔍 **Massage oil**
- 🔍 **Tickets to a movie, sports event, or concert**
- 🔍 **A disposable camera**

Be a Wallflower Inexpensive, preglued wallpaper borders come in wonderful, unusual patterns. They are now sold in large chain stores as well as specialty stores. Borders come in small rolls, and you can give the illusion of ribbon on wrapping paper just by adding a strip to your package. Use these borders with or without ribbons.

911 Emergency! Help! No Ribbon!! If you don't have enough ribbon to traditionally wrap around the whole box, take the length that you have and attach it to the corner surface of the box using double-sided or rolled tape to add a touch of whimsy. I've used shoelaces tied together, real ivy, scarves, men's ties (sorry, dear!), and even belts as ribbon substitutes.

I Can Get It for You Wholesale

You may never run out of ribbon if you can buy it at the right price! JKM Ribbon in West Berlin, New Jersey (800-767-3635), offers wired organza, chiffon, tulle, jute, metallic, moiré, and hand-dyed silk ribbons in a huge variety of colors. The price is right, and you can view samples at their Website (www.jkmribbon.com). Michaels, a retail chain with more than 500 stores, has fantastic ribbons at fantastic prices (www.michaels.com).

Nashville Wraps

Although this package design company has a $25 minimum, you get a big bang for your buck (800-547-9727). Ribbon, tissue paper, cellophane, boxes, bags, and gift wraps can be yours for terrific prices. I love their tulle floral ribbon ($2.50 for 25 yards). Their Website (www.nashvillewraps.com) (800-547-9727) should be gift wrapped!

Baby BOTHER

Holy Moley

Weaving ribbon is a fantasy touch that is so easy.

1   **Borrow a hole puncher from your 12-year-old son.**

2   **Place your gift in a bag without handles.**

3   **Pull the top of the bag together and punch two vertical holes about an inch from the top on both sides of the bag.**

4   **Fold down the top of the bag so that the top holes meet the bottom holes.**

5   **Weave your ribbon through the holes on either side and tie in two separate bows on the top.**

Variations on a Theme Punch holes intermittently across the top of the bag and weave the ribbon across, tying the bows on either side. You can also weave ribbon on a note card by punching holes across the top of the card.

I Left My Heart

Bellocchio, a tiny gem of a store in San Francisco (415-864-4048), sells the most magnificent antique, vintage, and modern ribbons that these eyes have ever seen. People actually buy these ribbons as gifts because they are so unique. Toby and Claudia scour small companies in Europe to fill every corner of their shop. The costume designer for the blockbuster movie *Titanic* actually found antique gilded rose ribbon here to use on the wardrobe. Eighteenth-century silk fabric is used as wrapping paper, as are other one-of-a-kind fabrics. And if it's boxes you're after . . . novelty shapes such as lemons, shrimp, olives, and cherries can be yours. (Their oyster design box is frequently used to wrap pearls.) New creations are constantly being added to the merchandise. There is actually a waiting list for their "scallopinkies"—pinking shears that cut scalloped edges on fabric. I would love to tie a velvet ribbon around this store and drag it to your hometown, but it's easier for you to visit their Website (www.bellocchio.com).

"Puff & Stuff"

Never throw out tissue paper. It's a wonderful tool that can make clothes come "alive." This idea works best with kids' clothes, but it also adds punch to adult sweaters, gloves, and tops.

- Before putting your present in a gift box, stuff the arms and body with tissue paper to the point that it could almost stand up on its own.
- Stuff it into a box.
- When the box is opened, the effect is as if the gift is being modeled.

I take a slightly different approach with baby clothes.

- Hang the gift on a mini hanger (which you can get from a store if you beg).
- Stuff the item with tissue paper.
- Put plastic from the cleaners over the hanger.
- Gather at the bottom, and tie with lots of ribbon.

Can you say P-R-E-C-I-O-U-S?

"The Gift Card Dilemma"

If you follow these foolproof instructions, you needn't worry that your gift card will slip out and that your boss will think that you got him those ugly slippers.

🔍 **Wrap your gift-card envelope with any kind of ribbon, as if *it* was a gift box.**

🔍 **Tie the ends of the ribbon to the gift.**

It's also a great way to wrap gift certificates and checks.

It's always a terrific treat to put dried flowers, rose petals, or herbs in gift-card envelopes. The Fredericksburg Herb Farm in Texas has wonderful offerings (800-259-HERB). You can also visit their Website (www.fredericksburgherbfarm.com).

Baby BOTHER

Farewell Hallmark! It's time to transfer the old name-game onto a gift card! You can use any piece of plain paper. Write the person's name multiple times, on an angle, on one side of the paper. Fold it in half, and it becomes a gift card (the empty side is on the inside). Having beautiful handwriting is a plus, but even if your scrawl is uneven, this presentation always works.

Before I wrap up this chapter, I have a personal confession to make. I'd like to tell you I got my job at one of the most prestigious news organizations on merit alone, but I don't think so. I think it's because I ***"bothered."***

"Tiffany Method"

A decade ago, I wrapped my on-camera demo tape to CNN in a big turquoise box from Tiffany's. I included a note that touted myself as an "unpolished gem." Now, I don't recommend the "Tiffany method" as a foolproof way to break into journalism, but I do recommend **"bothering"** to take those few extra minutes to set yourself apart from the rest.

"My Hero!"

In the "didn't work for me" department, I once put my voiceover tape in a hero sandwich, wrapped it in white deli paper, and sent it to an agent at the William Morris Agency with a note stating that he was my hero. I never heard from him—maybe he doesn't like meatballs!

We all know that it's the thought that counts. But it's also the wrapping!

Ooh & Aah Entertaining

You may think you can't hit a grand slam every time you entertain, but you know what? You don't have to. All it takes is one masterpiece per meal to win raves from your guests. Let me show you how.

As long as you hear oohs and aahs over that one unbelievable (yet easy) item you've created, you can feed the burnt roast to the dog and no one will be the wiser. This chapter will provide you with over 100 foolproof ideas for those memorable, edible moments. Here's one of them.

At the height of **Michael Jackson** mania, the Gloved One arrived at Swifty Lazar's Oscar bash at Spago with **Madonna** on his arm. After the excitement died down, all the guests could talk about were the mini golden chocolate Oscars ("dusted with real gold") that chef extraordinaire **Wolfgang Puck** had provided for each guest. One simple idea became the talk of the town.

To help you get ready for your standing ovation, I've divided these surefire hits into meal periods: **Brunch/Lunch, Cocktails and a Little Somethin', Seductive Sides, The Main Event, Kidz Stuff, The Grand Finale, Table Toppers,** and **One Size Fits All.** Choose one or two to add to your special repertoire, and get ready to take a bow.

Brunch/ Lunch

(My favorite meal, 'cuz you can eat the delicious leftovers the same day!)

The Ultimate Coffee Cake
Prepare a store-bought coffee cake mixture and bake it inside oversize overnproof coffee cups. (Make sure you keep a watchful eye on these babies, because they will bake faster than the directions advise!) Serve these "decaf" treats with a cinnamon stick on each saucer. And as if this isn't adorable enough, stick a cloth napkin in the handle of each cup.

Sundae Surprise
Remember your world before you knew about cellulite? When you went to your corner drugstore, not to buy diet pills but to have coffee ice cream with hot butterscotch sauce? I do. And because I salivate every time I see an empty parfait glass, I figure why not **"bother"** to use that sensory memory to entertain.

Layer granola, vanilla yogurt, and sliced strawberries in a parfait glass. For that extra little oomph, serve with a straw and a long ice cream spoon. You can also layer cold cereal and sliced fruit. The layers should be repeated twice for a breakfast of champions. Enjoy your guiltless sundae!

Smoked Salmon Pizza
You will need a pizza pan for maximum effect for this delicacy in the round. I got mine at Kmart for $7.99.

1. Buy frozen pizza dough.

2. Bake on the pizza pan according to package directions.

3. Cool completely.

4. Spread plain or flavored cream cheese over the crust, as if it were tomato sauce.

5. Place strips of smoked salmon on top of the cream cheese, as if it were mozzarella cheese.

6. Sprinkle fresh dill over your smoked salmon pizza.

7. Salivate and slice!

Bagel Mania
You don't have to be Jewish to order from David's Bagels in New City, New York (914-639-1664). They create a spectacular oversize bagel

sandwich in the shape of a letter or number that can serve up to 40 people. If you don't live in the area, they will FedEx the bagel. It's worth the **"bother"** and the expense. Perhaps your local bagel shop would like to expand their repertoire and include this gigantic gimmick.

Cannes Film Festival Morning Madness

Most years in the month of May, I head to the Mediterranean to cover the world's most glamorous film festival. I've had the privilege of interviewing superstars like Tom Cruise, but I've also had the unfortunate privilege of paying $50 for a cappuccino and a croissant. The hype is marked up, and so are the prices. So when I was invited by Miramax Studios to have brunch on their private yacht, I said yes and ate everything in sight. But what I remember most besides receiving no check was the way the chef served the dry cereal . . . yeah, the raisin bran. He served five different varieties in oversize serving bowls from Provence. You mixed and matched your flavors, but the cardboard boxes were banished. Muslix was never so marvelous.

Twisted French Toast

As long as we're in France, let's serve some French toast with a French twist. Whenever I'm in a flea market, I collect unusual serving pieces. When I was judging Miss Teen USA in Wichita, Kansas, I hit pay dirt. I found a huge laminated tray with a map of Paris on it for $2.99. Natch, whenever I serve this tantalizing toast, it's on my Paris tray. You can easily re-create that feeling by finding a cloth napkin with French writing on it, or a napkin that boasts the colors of the French flag. You can serve your toast in a basket atop the napkin. Watch out Julia Child! *Bon appétit.*

Morning Martini Mania

Martini glasses can be more than just stirred or shaken. Instead of taking that dollop of tuna salad and dumping it on a plate . . . dump it into a martini glass. Slide two green olives and a whole cocktail onion on a toothpick and place it on an angle in the glass. You can also use chicken salad, crabmeat, or even lobster chunks if you've hit the Lotto!

Baby BOTHER

Popover Plants

Don't skip this one—it's much easier than it looks. Kitchen-supply companies sell bake-ready, mini flowerpots. Prepare your favorite popover mix, and pour the batter into the pots, until they're ¾ full. After they cool, place a flower without a stem on top of the popover before serving. This idea is sure to grow on you.

Get a Handle on Your Omelet

I'm not asking you to give up your favorite egg pan . . . but after your cooking is complete, transfer your omelet to an individual antique skillet (which can be found at most flea markets) instead of a plate. The look is more fun when the pans don't match. If you don't like to be caught with egg on your face, these inexpensive pans work for hash browns, grits, or whatever you're craving.

Baby BOTHER

Edible Bread Basket

You can find raw bread dough in the refrigerated section of most major supermarkets. Bake according to package directions, but mold the dough over a heat-resistant bowl that has been placed face-down on a cookie sheet. Remove from the heat, and let cool for at least ½ hour. Gently remove the bread from the bowl. Turn it over and congratulate yourself for making an edible bread bowl. Fill this unusual serving piece with savory muffins, scones, and bagels. This is a fun idea, no matter whom you decide to break bread with. You can even make smaller bread bowls to hold different flavors of jellies and jams!

Cocktails and a Little Somethin'

Man (and woman) does not live by liquid alone. Whenever you invite guests over for the pre-verbial "drink," make sure to offer a little somethin' from the food department.

Creative Crudités

Don't you dare just plop some cut veggies on a plate and call it a day. Look around, and you'll find just the right unusual container to present your crunchy munchies.

- 🔍 A large terra-cotta pot and a tiny one for your dip
- 🔍 An opened lunch box
- 🔍 A large skillet
- 🔍 A small wooden window box

🔍 **A large soup tureen with the dip in the ladle**

🔍 **A hollowed-out round loaf of bread for tall items, such as carrots, asparagus, string beans, or cucumber strips**

🔍 **A picnic basket**

🔍 **A small suitcase (no, really!)**

Be sure to line any container with plastic wrap and overlapping long lettuce leaves, such as red-tipped romaine, to make the crudités look lush.

Baby BOTHER Hollow out a head of radicchio, or a small head of Bibb lettuce, to make an ad hoc bowl for your dip. Now go skinny-dipping!

The Shrimp Boats Are Comin'

I always say, Why serve shrimp on a plate when you can arrange them in a shrimp boat? Okay, I don't always say that, but it takes the same amount of time to do both. I found a wooden boat at Cost Plus in west L.A. for $5.99, but there are "props" all around your home—you don't have to go out and buy them. I've even served shrimp and sushi on a platter lined with fishing net. You can buy an adorable fish mold for $4 from Bridge Kitchenware (212-838-1901). Toast some white bread (which you shouldn't eat, but it's a wonderful design tool). Press the mold onto the toast, and you have a whole school of fishies to befriend your shrimp.

Serve your cocktail sauce in a hollowed-out lemon. (Make sure to stabilize the bottom so that it doesn't ooze out onto your new white carpet.)

Peanuttiest

Betcha can't eat just one caramelized peanut. Spread the contents of a bag of shelled peanuts onto a greased baking sheet. Melt ½ stick of butter mixed with 2 tablespoons of brown sugar and drizzle over the nuts. Bake at 350°F for 15 minutes, turning halfway through. Cool and refrain from eating them all before your guests arrive. Serve them in an empty peanut butter jar!

Spooning

For my money, **Audrey Hepburn** was the quintessential Hollywood movie star (if you don't know who she is, put down this book, go to your nearest video store, and rent *Breakfast at Tiffany's*). I had the privilege of breaking bread with her at a luncheon at the United Nations, where she planned the menu. To start the meal, a beautiful plate with eight antique little spoons was set down on the tables. On each little spoon was one diver scallop with herb broth. Talk about controlled portions! Throughout the years, I have re-created this idea using little mounds of curried tuna (just add a little curry powder to your favorite tuna recipe). I used inexpensive dessert spoons until I found enamel demitasse spoons at a flea market in Kutztown, Pennsylvania. Very elegant . . . very Audrey.

Meatball Mania

Prepare your favorite meatball, veal ball, or turkey ball recipe. When you are ready to serve these marvelous morsels . . . use a bread bowl. Carve a circle out of the top of a round, crusty bread. Carefully lift the top off the bread and hollow it out with your hands. Pour the meatballs into your bread bowl, and put the top back on to keep these babies warm. Mamma mia!

Hollywood Cocktail Parties

These shindigs are always on the cutting edge of food trends. A look back at past premiere menus becomes a who's who of hors d'oeuvres.

- In the '70s, quiche reigned supreme.
- In the '80s, sun-dried tomatoes and sushi held the spotlight.
- In the early '90s, pasta salad and kiwi took center stage.

And now we're going back to basics with feel-good food. But one classic hors d'oeuvre that never goes out of style is caviar! Don't be afraid of the price. I use Romanoff in most of my recipes, which costs about $7.98 a jar and serves up to 50 people. The following two caviar recipes are superstars, so please don't be intimidated by the main ingredient.

"EZ" Buckwheat Pancakes with Caviar and Crème Fraîche

Go to your grocery store and buy a package of buckwheat pancake mix. Don't tell anybody. Follow the EZ directions on the box, but make the pancakes mini (about 2 inches wide). After they cool, put a teaspoon of crème fraîche (or sour cream or nonfat sour cream or plain yogurt) on each mini pancake. Add a small drained dollop of caviar to each one . . . then put on your sunglasses and go Hollywood! (The plain pancakes can be frozen for last-minute situations.)

Caviar Pie This is my most requested "ooh and aah." Every time I make it, I wish that I could just put it in the photocopy machine! But then reality hits, and I'm back at the stove.

Here are the pie and filling ingredients:

> *1 ready-made pie crust (you can find it in your supermarket's frozen section)*
>
> *8 ounces whipped cream cheese*
>
> *¼ cup mayonnaise (you can use nonfat mayo if you prefer)*
>
> *3 teaspoons grated white onion*
>
> *3 teaspoons Worcestershire sauce*
>
> *3 teaspoons fresh lemon juice*

1. Prepare the pie crust according to the package instructions and let it cool.

2. In a bowl, mix all of the other ingredients with a large spoon.

3. Pour the filling into the pie crust and set aside.

Here are the garnishes:

> *3 teaspoons drained black (inexpensive) caviar*
>
> *3 chopped hard-boiled egg yolks*
>
> *3 tablespoons finely chopped red onion*
>
> *2 generous handfuls of chopped parsley*

1. Don't be afraid! You are not going to ruin this!

2. Sprinkle the parsley around the outer edge of the pie (directly beside the crust).

3   Sprinkle the egg around the inner edge of the parsley (creating concentric circles).

4   Sprinkle the onion around the inner edge of the egg.

5   Now you are left with a small circle at the center of your pie . . . but not for long.

6   Fill the circle with your drained caviar.

7   Refrigerate for at least an hour before serving.

Now you have your pie in the sky!

*Seductive Sides *

Side dishes are often afterthoughts. But I'm here to boost their egos and bring them onto the front burner of your recipe planning.

Say Good-bye to Fancy-Schmancy Serving Platters

Let your food do the holding! First, there are the obvious creations that I call "like kinds." For instance, you can make **squash soup in a squash bowl.** Cut your squash in half, scoop out the pulp, and serve your soup in your newly made squash bowl.

Baby BOTHER

If you want to *"bother"* a little more, you can make a squash bowl with a top on it that will keep your soup warm! Carve a round circle in the top of a whole squash as if you were carving a pumpkin. Be sure to leave about ½ inch around the circumference of the squash. Once you have hollowed out the vegetable and cleaned off the top, you get to cover your bowl with your top! You can also use rice, couscous, or mashed potatoes in this bowl.

Now that you've got the cut-and-scoop method down pat, here are some other ideas to ensure that you won't be washing any dishes!

Orange Fill with orange sherbet, orange sorbet, orange-flavored rice, orange mousse, etc.

Lemon Fill with lemon butter, lemon wedges, lemon mousse, lemon sorbet, or even water as a finger bowl!

Melon Fill with different kinds of melon or even strawberries, raspberries, blueberries, or mini scoops of rainbow sherbet.

Peppers Fill with peas, baby carrots, orzo, or creamed spinach. (You can make your Aunt Sophie's recipe for creamed spinach, or simply use Stouffer's or Pepperidge Farm's and just add a little nutmeg or fresh pepper.)

Use these edible dishes to hold silverware as well as food. Just make sure that the vegetable is sturdy enough so that it doesn't topple over. They work well with your plastic cutlery collection!

Speaking of Collections
Check your Sunday newspaper, then flee your home for your local flea and antiques markets. I have found so many treasures (under $5) that are just perfect for serving unique side dishes. Some of them may even be stashed in a storage box in your basement!

Small old milk bottles: Perfect for pouring sour cream over your baked potatoes or holding single servings of mashed potatoes.

Small antique skillets: Great as bread and butter plates or as individual serving dishes for a combo of sides such as wild rice, sugar snap peas, and pureed sweet potatoes.

Old salad colanders: This is a unique way to serve greens, but keep a plate underneath. If you are inclined to opt for a plain ol' salad plate, pop it in the freezer before serving. It will keep your greens *soooo* crisp.

Army mess kits: As long as you're not using Granny's fine china, this is a fun way to serve sides.

At the Santa Monica, California, antique market (held on the fourth Sunday of every month), it seems as if one out of every 50 shoppers is a star. But finding all the treasures is not a perk written into their contracts. Recently, **Geena Davis** had her long, lithe fingers wrapped around a funky old ice bucket that I really wanted to serve ice cream in. After watching her hem and haw for five minutes, I simply told her that I really, really wanted it. And she handed it over, just as graciously as she gave her Oscar acceptance speech. So don't be afraid to be aggressive during your treasure hunts. If you feel passionate, speak up. Most shoppers will understand.

Vegetable Sundae Surprise

Get out your parfait glasses and start layering vegetable combinations that complement one another:

- Peas, carrots, mashed potatoes
- Spinach and ratatouille
- Broccoli and pine nuts
- Macaroni and cheese with green peppers
- Vegetable mousses

If you serve this with a long ice cream spoon, people will be sure to finish their vegetables.

In the Can
Use canned potato sticks to form numbers, initials, or names on a plate for personalized entertaining. If you want to improve your eyesight, you can also do this with carrot sticks.

Cucumber Cups
One of the reasons why the phenomenal spa The Golden Door is so popular with Hollywood folk, is because of its chef, Michel Stroot. He can even make cucumber taste like crème brûlée. (Okay, maybe I was hallucinating, but the man is pure magic.) His presentation of mesclun salad is so simple, yet it always wins raves.

1. Peel the skin off a very long cucumber.

2. Peel about 10 thin strips of cucumber.

3. Place a handful of lettuce on your plate; try to keep it in the shape of a ball.

4   Place strips of cucumber one by one around the ball of lettuce, building upward until the strips form a wall around the greens.

5   The cukes will actually stick to one another . . . no need for a glue gun!

Baby BOTHER

Belgian Fries Now that we've pigged out on lettuce and cucumbers, we deserve a little treat. The delicious french fries in Belgium are not served in cardboard containers with an "M" insignia. They are wrapped in newspaper, which absorbs the oil. This presentation is fun and functional.

1   Cut a large triangle (about a foot long) out of newspaper.

2   With the point of the triangle facing down, place your fries in the top center of the newspaper.

3   Wrap the newspaper edges around your fries, tucking the pointy part inside.

4   You can use different sections of your newspaper, depending on the crowd: sports, financial, movies, etc.

Attention Asparagus Shoppers Serve them "standing up." If you grill or steam them, and they are not limp, be proud. Stand them up and wrap a blanched leek around your bunch. If you can't balance your veggies, stand them vertically in a glass, a vase, or hollowed-out bread. Now salute them.

The Main Event

All courses are created equal, so don't fret over this one . . . just have fun with it!

Not Your Mother's Meat Loaf

Here's some comfort food with a twist.

1. Prepare your favorite meat loaf recipe, but instead of using ye ol' loaf pan, bake it in two round cake pans.

2. Let cool.

3. Assemble as if it were a layer cake.

4. Frost the top of the first layer with mashed potatoes, add the bottom layer, and frost the whole shebang.

5. You can even add candles and serve this little piece of comfort on a cake plate.

Portobello Plates The bigger the better . . .

These work well when topped with any kind of fish or vegetable.

1. Rinse your oversize portobello mushrooms and pat them very dry.

2. Transfer these babies to a baking sheet.

3. Drizzle with olive oil.

4   Add a pinch of kosher salt, fresh pepper, and herbs
    (dried or fresh).

5   Bake for 12 minutes at 400°F, and your plates are ready.

6   To reheat, place your plate and topping in heavy-duty
    tin foil for 10 to 15 minutes at 400°F.

Do not . . . I repeat . . . *Do not* . . . put your mushrooms in the dishwasher.

Baby BOTHER

Luscious Lamb and Friends

I am including this lamb recipe because it is foolproof
and delicious . . . but it's the "friends" that make this
a "Why Bother?" (and I ain't talkin' **Jennifer Aniston**).

1   In a glass dish, marinate a trimmed, butterflied leg of
    lamb in 1 cup of honey or maple syrup, 1 cup of soy sauce,
    8 cloves of minced garlic, a few shakes of pepper, and
    10 sprigs of rosemary for at least 2 hours (you may
    substitute 2 teaspoons of dried rosemary for the fresh).

2   Grill or broil for 12 minutes per side . . . but don't go
    and watch your soap opera, because you have to baste
    your little lamb every 5 minutes.

3   Remove from the heat.

4   When cool, slice on a diagonal. The meat should be
    charred on the outside and pink on the inside.

Okay . . . here's where the friends come in.

- Right before serving, toast a couple of pieces of white bread.

- Locate any animal cookie cutters you might have around the kitchen (barnyard animals, zoo creatures, etc.).

- Press the mold into the toast, and brush your toast animals with olive oil infused with garlic.

- Fill the bottom of your platter with parsley, which will look like grass.

- Place your animals out to graze on the parsley and fill the rest of the platter with your lamb. Mary . . . eat your heart out!

Sandwich in the Round

Slice an oversize, round crusty bread in half, horizontally. On the bottom piece of bread, build the sandwich with your favorite ingredients. Reassemble the top and serve whole. When you are ready to eat, cut this humongous sandwich in wedges.

Kreative Kabobs

Instead of using metal or wooden skewers while grilling or broiling, think herbs! Use a stalk of rosemary (at least 7 inches) to thread lamb, fish, chicken, or steak and all the fixins'. But you must first make a small hole in each item to ensure that it will thread smoothly. And if you really wanna rough it . . . you can also use small twigs as skewers, but make sure you're not cooking them directly over high flames.

Play With Your Food! I know we're not supposed to be talking about dessert yet, but trust me, it works. **Michael Douglas** and **Catherine Zeta-Jones** share a lot . . . including their birthdays. To mark the milestone one year, Michael received a cake in the shape of a giant golf ball, while Catherine's was molded into a pair of tap shoes. But sweets aside, this molding method can also be used with your main courses.

I know you've always been taught not to play with your food, but hey, now you're the adult. I've formed egg salad into the shape of a tennis racket and sprinkled chopped parsley as the strings. I've shaped tuna salad and chopped liver into block-letter initials and crabmeat salad into numbers. Disposable gloves come in handy for this project, but if you don't have 'em, a good hand washing will do.

Kidz Stuff *

Say good-bye to picky little eaters. A couple of playful devices will have them eating right out of your hand (or off a plate if you so desire).

Ketchup and Mustard Art

Pour your favorite brand of ketchup and mustard into separate pointed plastic squeeze bottles. Now, squeeze:

- Happy faces on burgers
- Birthday numbers on hot dogs
- Kidz names on cheeseburgers
- Phrases on the plate (such as "eat your spinach or no dessert")

Milky Way

They won't even know that they're drinking something that is good for them! Pour chocolate milk into an ice cube tray (filling it up only ¾ of the way to allow for expansion). Then simply add a couple of these chocolate cubes to a regular glass of milk, and watch it disappear.

Don't Be a Square

When I was little, cookie cutters only came in the shapes of hearts, stars, circles, and Santa (if you could find him). Now, the sky's the limit. Practically anything from Teletubbies to telephones can be found in a mold. So stop being a square. Serve a tuna sandwich in the shape of Barney; make an egg salad daisy and a roast beef Pokémon. Every meal can be an edible playland.

Coneheads

Ice cream cones are not just for ice cream anymore.

1. Scoop cottage cheese, tuna salad, egg salad, or your choice of fillings inside and atop your packaged flat-bottomed wafer cone.

2. Substitute parsley or chopped nuts for candy sprinkles. Don't worry . . . these cones won't drip!

For dessert, try making cupcake conesfor your little cupcakes. Here's what you'll need:

1 box of flat-bottomed wafer cones
1 muffin tray
1 package of cupcake or muffin mix
1 container of icing

1   Place your flat-bottomed wafer cones into the spaces of a muffin tray.

2   Prepare the cupcake mix according to the package directions.

3   Pour the batter into the individual cones (fill them halfway).

4   Bake for the time specified in the package directions.

5   Frost your cupcake cones and decorate with sprinkles or candy pieces. Make happy faces, or let your own little happy faces decorate their own cupcake cones.

The Grand Finale *

Next to "I love you" and "peace on earth," I think "baked on the premises" is my favorite phrase. But since we all have busy premises, I'll show you ways around that. In showbiz, we say, "You're only as good as your last show." Keep in mind that dessert is your last show, so let's make it spectacular.

So You Don't Own Limoges Dessert Plates?

Who cares? Take any plain white plate (plastic included) and place your dessert in the center. Crisscross a spoon and a fork at the edge of the plate. Sprinkle cocoa over and around the silverware, including the sides of the plate. Carefully lift up the utensils (don't sneeze!) and you have a sensational presentation: a cocoa shadow box!

The Icing on the Cake

What's better in life than licking the icing out of the bowl? Okay, so it's not #1 on your list, but I'm sure it's up there. And since that bowl is already washed and put back in the cupboard by the time your guests arrive, let them have their cake and eat it too.

Baby BOTHER

Slice a delicious homemade round cake (or a store-bought one) into wedges. Frost all surfaces of each piece, transforming it into a whole mini cake. Keep in mind that fat-free icings now exist on our planet! Carrot cake works well with fat-free cream cheese icing, and try mocha cake with cappuccino icing.

Doilies Are Not Just for Granny

Buy a plain cake, or make one yourself. Place a doily over the cake so that it covers all of the edges. Sprinkle a healthy amount of confectioners' sugar over the top of the doily, until the entire top of the cake is covered. (Make sure you are in a wind-free environment when you attempt this project. If you live in Chicago, close the windows.) Lift the doily carefully off the cake and pat yourself on the back for a job well done if you are left with a beautiful design on top of your cake. If not, just wipe off the sugar and try again. It's okay—Rome wasn't built in a day.

Puzzling Cupcakes

Use a store-bought icing tube to write a message letter by letter on each cupcake. Serve them in order, or mix them up and have your guests decipher the code.

Individual Cozy Pumpkin Pie

Hollow out mini pumpkins, until you are left with just the shell. Prepare your favorite recipe for pumpkin pie (I like to add chocolate chunks to mine). Pour your batter 2/3 of the way into your mini pumpkins. Bake and serve with a mini scoop of ice cream on the side.

Shapely, Hot, and Sweet

And I'm not talking about **Ricky Martin**. . . . Cut a store-bought sheet cake (or one you baked on the premises) into big initials or numbers that represent your celebration. Frost the shapes and drizzle warm caramel or chocolate sauce over the top and sides.

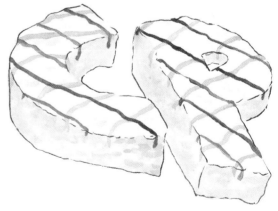

Baby BOTHER Garden Cake

Ice a sheet cake with white icing. Design a large flower for the top; use licorice for the stem, mint for the leaves, kiwi for the center, and cut strawberries for the petals. Sprinkle edible rose petals over the rest of the cake. (Order them from the Herb Lady, 616-674-3879, or use organic pansies.)

Big BOTHER Let's take our Garden Cake one step further. Buy a piece of sod from your local nursery. Place it over a small dessert table, or cut it to fit a large tray. Find a plate that is the same size as your cake. Put your cake on the plate, then place the plate on top of the sod. Trust me, this idea will grow on you. And if you want to go crazy . . . serve your coffee in a metal watering can.

Baby BOTHER

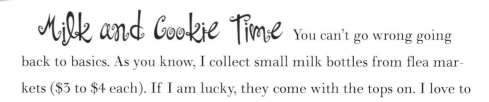

Picture Perfect Pastry
I still can't program my VCR. But if you are a computer whiz kid, www.kopykake.com can show you how to transfer an actual photo onto a cake or cookie. I take the easy way out and sometimes order photo cookies from Eric Borrer (212-989-6351). They are delicious and shipped nicely all over the U.S. (The cost is $1.50 per unwrapped cookie; $2.50 per cookie wrapped in cellophane. There is a $100 minimum, and Eric accepts only checks.) And this time it's okay to bite off your mother-in-law's head! (Even though I adore mine!)

Milk and Cookie Time
You can't go wrong going back to basics. As you know, I collect small milk bottles from flea markets ($3 to $4 each). If I am lucky, they come with the tops on. I love to

serve warm cookies and individual milk bottles to my guests. (They can drink directly from the bottle without getting in trouble!)

I Scream, You Scream
Serve ice cream inside small milk bottles, and give each guest long ice cream spoons. Be sure to freeze the bottles first. You can also use them for milk chocolate mousse or chocolate pudding.

Bountiful Beach Pails
Even if I use my best china, I think dessert can always be fun and informal. I like to serve frozen yogurt or ice cream in beach pails and use a sand shovel as the ice cream scooper.

Baby BOTHER

Sorbet Serving
Buy some inexpensive wooden paint palettes from your local art store to use as plates. Scoop different flavors of sorbet onto the palettes as if they were paints. Van Gogh would be proud.

The party for the premiere of *The Age of Innocence* was as magnificent as the film. For dessert, sorbet was served in fantastic floral shapes, such as tulips, roses, and lilies. The sorbets were shipped from St. Claire Ice Cream in Norwalk, Connecticut (203-853-4774), where you can get them too. St. Claire's also provided the sorbets that were in the movie. For the launching of *Sex*, Madonna's provocative book, St. Claire's was asked to come up with sorbets in the shape of body parts. They declined, but did provide banana-shaped ices. This company offers 15 scrumptious flavors and can make any shape you want. Flavors packed by the dozen are $13 plus shipping. No credit cards, please. And, by the way, you won't be frozen out! Packed in dry ice, these little wonders arrive in perfect condition.

Sorbet Frutti-Tutti

Scoop out the insides of an orange, lemon, lime, coconut, or pineapple, and fill with sorbet. Place the top back on, wrap in plastic, and freeze until you are ready to serve.

Elegant Grapes

Grapes are good for more than just making wine. Here's how to dress 'em up. You will need 2 pounds of seedless grapes and 12 ounces of white, dark, or milk chocolate.

1. Make sure your grapes are very, very dry.

2. Melt your chocolate in a microwave or a double boiler.

3. Dip small bunches of grapes into the chocolate and place them on wax paper to set.

4. Put them in the fridge for at least 12 hours.

5. Serve these elegant treats.

If you're antichocolate, dip your grapes in a bath of egg whites and then dust them with granulated sugar! Chill as directed above.

Birthday Plate
Even the water at the Four Seasons in Beverly Hills tastes divine. For birthdays, the pastry chef and Charles Hawkins, the concierge, design a wonderful yet easy treat that awaits you in your hotel room. Place one piece of cake on a plate. With a store-bought icing tube, write "Happy Birthday" and the name of your guest on the plate. You can do this at home for any occasion.

It's the Pits
Unfortunately, I can't teach you how to make the intricate watermelon sculptures that were done for the premiere of *The Little Mermaid*. They re-created the film's underwater world using the summer treat. But with just four cuts, you can make your spirit swim.

1 Cut your melon in half horizontally.

2 Scoop out the center, reserving the fruit, to create an empty shell.

3 Scallop the edges by making 1-inch crisscross cuts.

4 Fill your melon bowl with berries, cherries, melon . . . You can also add scoops of sorbet if you are serving it immediately.

5 For a lush look, add a generous portion of mint that overflows your bowl.

Get a Handle on Your Basket

This presentation will take five minutes more than the watermelon bowls. It sounds complicated, but it's not—I promise.

1. Make a horizontal cut in your melon, leaving 2 inches attached in the center.

2. Make two vertical cuts from the top of the watermelon that intersect your horizontal cut to form two large L's.

3. Lift out both of those L's and scoop.

4. Now you have a handle on your basket; fill it with nature's best.

You can do this presentation with cantaloupes and honeydews and even with lemons and limes.

Just Peachy

When serving peaches, plums, or apples, place a single fruit on a plate. Put two leaves on either side of the fruit . . . and it's as if Mother Nature was your food stylist.

Not a Creature Was Stirring

A chocolate-covered spoon is a stirring addition to your piping-hot coffee. Melt two chocolate squares (you can use unsweetened if you like) in your microwave or over a double boiler. Then coat the spoon (except the handles) with the melted chocolate. Place them on wax paper to set. Refrigerate for at least 12 hours before using.

There is a large selection of flavored chocolates (and coffees). . . . Go for it! I like to use mocha-almond-mint. It releases such a wonderful flavor when stirred into coffee.

Good Humor Pour your favorite mixture of piña colada, daiquiri, or margarita into an ice-pop mold. Choose a designated driver if someone wants seconds!

Jell-O Make your Jell-O according to the package directions, but instead of letting it set in a glass, pour it into a scooped-out orange. Refrigerate. Serve this old standby in a new way.

Big BOTHER

Dessert Pizza Yes, you read it correctly. This "sweet pizza" is definitely worth the effort. You will need a pizza pan for maximum effect. I bought mine at Kmart for $7.99.

1. Buy a roll of premade sugar cookie dough (you'll find it in the refrigerated section of your supermarket).

2. Spray your pizza pan with a nonstick coating such as Pam.

3. Press or roll the sugar cookie dough onto the pizza pan as if it were pizza crust.

4. Bake according to the package directions and allow the crust to cool.

5. In a small bowl, mix an 8-ounce tub of whipped cream cheese with 2 tablespoons of vanilla extract and sugar to taste. (Of course, you can substitute artificial sweetener and nonfat cream cheese.)

6 Spread the mixture on top of the crust, as if it were tomato sauce spread on a pizza.

7 Let your taste buds be your guide when adding toppings to your dessert pizza: raspberries, grapes, strawberries, raisins, walnuts, blueberries, chocolate chips, pineapple chunks, canned cherries, etc.

Table Toppers

To top off your incredible edibles, let's give a little airtime to the table they're sitting on. But first let me say "You must erase all preconceived notions about how your grandmother set the table." The only rule to abide by is to have fun.

Table Wear

Call me a prude, but I really don't care for "see-thru" clothing. But "see-thru" tablecloths really get me cooking on all four burners. Transparent plastic ones come in all shapes and sizes and are so versatile: use them as a laminate for what's displayed underneath. Here are some other ideas:

- **A Sunday paper** (for a Sunday brunch)
- **The comics** (for kidz)
- **An Italian flag** (for an Italian feast)
- **Baby pictures** (for a birthday dinner)
- **Children's artwork**
- **Autumn leaves**
- **Black-and-white postcards**
- **Posters**
- **Old letters**
- **Magazine articles**

Your list can be as endless as your interests!

Wearable Tablecloths

A shawl draped on an angle over a table is an interesting look, as are silk scarves. (Don't worry . . . your dry cleaner can do amazing things.)

The Layered Look Different textures layered over one another always hold my interest. Old tapestries, antique curtains, even bed sheets, quilts, burlap bags, and blankets will work.

The Buffet Table

Now that all of these tablecloth options are part of your arsenal, let's put them to work. First, get out a couple of thick telephone books (no, not to call a caterer). The books will give your table different height levels when you cover them with the cloth of your choice. Place the books on the back third of your table. Drape them with the fabrics to create different serving stations that not only look professional but also make it easy for your guests to fend for themselves.

The Prop Department

On page 62, we dissected the anatomy of sensational floral and creative centerpieces. But in addition to these fabulous focal points . . . there is always room for some playful props.

- **For brunch, a couple of alarm clocks**
- **For an outdoor summer lunch, flower-filled water cans for each guest**
- **For a barbecue, empty baked beans cans as vases**

Flea Market Finds

One woman's junk is another woman's serving platter. No matter what planet, country, or city I'm in, I always scour the local antiques markets. I love to use this old kid's stove to serve some goodies.

Nature can provide her own props . . .

- Rose petals
- Interesting leaves and pinecones to scatter around your table
- Ivy or eucalyptus becomes spectacular when circling each place setting
- Trailing ivy makes a romantic napkin ring
- Extra-large leaves look enchanting when used as place mats

Here's one for Ripley's: A hostess I know with a lot of funny bones sprinkled Beano capsules over the table when she was serving gassy chili. Anything goes when it's appropriate for your guests.

For the premiere of *The Color of Money*, starring **Paul Newman** and **Tom Cruise** (my favorites!), fake paper money with their pictures on it was scattered all over green felt tables. To me, that was worth a million.

Table Manners
(Or how not to stain your great-grandmother's antique tablecloth!)

Scrub a Dub The next time you pass a towel outlet with a sale sign in the window, park and pay . . . for all the washcloths that you can afford.

At the end of your dinner party:

1. Fill your sink or a pail with about a gallon of water.

2. Add 4 tablespoons of almond essence, lavender oil, lemon extract, or rose water.

3. Add the washcloths and let them soak for at least a minute.

4. Squeeze out 90 percent of the excess moisture.

5. Fold or roll them and put them in the microwave for one minute.

6. Offer them on a tray or in a basket or bucket to your guests as refreshing finger towels.

Community Finger Bowls These are fun and save the upholstery from barbecue sauce stains. Fill an oversize bowl with tepid water, cut-up lemons, and blossoms (like gardenias or roses). Place the bowl in the center of the table and let the cleaning begin. No splashing allowed!

One Size Fits All

Here are a couple of round-the-clock ideas that will work at any time of day. Have fun mixing and matching accordingly.

When it Rains, It Pours!

Here's an idea that takes approximately 16 seconds. Pour orange juice, lemonade, or apple cider from its plastic container into a wine carafe (which can cost you as little as

$2.99), and top it off with the corresponding fruit. If you are serving orange juice, stick an orange on top; for apple cider—you guessed it—an apple; and for lemonade . . . a watermelon! (Only kidding.)

Butter as an Accessory

I haven't had butter in my refrigerator for at least a decade, but since this is not a diet book, and you can be so creative with this wicked substance, I've decided to include it.

Baby BOTHER

Flavored Butter

Take the butter out of your fridge. When it becomes pliable, place it in a small bowl. Puree or mash some fresh fruit. Using the back of a spoon, blend the butter with the fruit. Use anyone of the following flavors:

- **Strawberry**
- **Raspberry**
- **Banana**
  (wonderful for brunch)
- **Blueberry**
- **Melted chocolate**

- **Lemon**
  (great for fish)
- **Rosemary**
- **Tarragon**
- **Garlic**
- **Mint**

If you don't have fresh fruit, add ½ teaspoon of jelly or jam to each stick.

Baby BOTHER

Herb Butter

Unwrap your stick of butter and cut it into equal pats (about ¼ inch thick). Press a piece of herb into the center of each pat. Put the pats on a plate and refrigerate. This method works well with parsley, mint, sage, rosemary, and peppercorns.

Shapely and Sinful

High cholesterol delivered in the shape of a half-moon, heart, or star lessens the blow a bit. Let your butter stand at room temperature until soft. Then spread it on wax paper so that it is ½ inch thick. Put it back in the fridge to harden. When it has hardened, press a cookie cutter or mold into the butter and remove your "butter shape" with a spatula. Transfer to a serving plate and keep cool until you are ready to serve this shapely spread.

Designer Ice

Pour any liquid that does not contain alcohol into your ice cube tray. You can either add the flavored ice to the same beverage (tea cubes in iced tea) or mix and match (cranberry juice cubes in orange juice). You can also make milk and chocolate milk ice cubes (which makes milk much more appealing for little kidz and adult kidz too).

For Adult Kidz Only Add red heart-shaped cubes to champagne. Add a drop or two of crème de cassis to a pitcher of water (if you use too much cassis, the water will not freeze). Pour the solution into your mold.

This **designer** ice even dresses up tap water. Add the following to your ice cubes while they are still in a liquid state.

- A sprig of mint
- A thin lemon slice
- A thin lime slice
- Zest of an orange
- A raspberry
- Edible flowers such as nasturtium or pansies

In a large clear glass or plastic pitcher, this effect is magical.

The X-Files **movie premiere bash** in Tinseltown was X-cellent. After the screening, the 1,300 guests entering a Santa Monica airport hangar were met by giant X's made out of ice. Ice sculptures are usually very difficult to make at home, but not this one. It's just a Baby Bother.

1   Cut off the top of an empty gallon plastic orange juice container.

2   Place a bottle of vodka in the center of the container.

3   Fill the container with water, leaving 1 inch at the top.

4   Evenly stuff flowers, leaves, peppers, vegetables, fruits, or herbs into the water surrounding the bottle.

5   Place the whole contraption in the freezer.

6   Freeze overnight.

7   About ½ hour before you are ready to serve, remove the container from the freezer.

8   Let it stand for about 10 minutes.

9   Peel and/or cut the sides of the plastic container away from the ice.

10   You have a beautiful frozen vodka ice sculpture.

Although this sculpture will melt very slowly, be sure to put a plate underneath when serving. When you are pouring the vodka, use a cloth to protect your hands from the ice.

Bodacious Bowls

If you are not a vodka drinker and would rather serve bodacious berries in a sumptuous sculpture, follow the directions above, but substitute a small bowl within a larger bowl for the vodka bottle in an orange juice container. Crisscross masking tape over the tops of both bowls while the ice is setting.

ProKitchen (888-485-7824) sells expensive but easy-to-use ice molds in any shape you can imagine. A mermaid, a swan, a bride and groom, and an ice sculpture punch bowl will set you back $39.95 for each item. ProKitchen is pro-credit card.

Pansy Under Glass

I came across this trick idea by accident, but hey, it's the bottom line that counts. Take a pansy and press it against the outside bottom of a moist glass. It should stick to the surface easily. Use the glass for transparent liquids like water, white wine, or champagne. Now, every time you sip, you'll smile.

And after your last guest has left, sit back, relax, and listen carefully: you should still be able to hear the sounds of _oohs and aahs._

Home "Suite" Home

stop stealing hotel towels; steal their ideas!

Relax, I'm not trying to get you arrested. I'm just trying to pack your suitcase with loads of special touches, the same ones that have enhanced the lives of celebrities when they travel outside of their gated estates! Star-studded hideaways, five-diamond resorts, and quaint country inns spend millions of dollars a year "bothering" to make your stay with them more comfortable. In many cases, consultants are hired to ensure those terrific amenities. Hurray for the stars, but how does this help you? Well, there are tons of ideas that you can "borrow" from these homes away from home—interesting concepts that you can incorporate into your own lifestyle easily and inexpensively. This chapter offers you a worldwide tour . . . a boarding pass to the good life. And in case your bags begin to feel a little heavy, I've stuffed your luggage with some descriptive destinations, so you can visualize these ideas in their original habitat! *Why Bother? Why Not!* I've already saved you the airfare.

Windsor Court

New Orleans, Louisiana

504-596-4513

www.preferredhotels.com

"Do you want more time in your morning?"

There'll be no indecision and fretting in front of your suitcase here. The Windsor Court slips the next day's weather under your door before bedtime, so you can lay out your clothes accordingly. Since there's no bellhop in your home, hop to it yourself. Find out tomorrow's weather and save time in the morning. It may be just 10 minutes a day, but hey, I'll take an extra hour a week!

Four Seasons Hotel

Chicago, Illnois

312-280-8800

800-332-3442

www.fourseasons.com

"Beating jet lag and curing homesickness during a holiday"

Just because celebs are sprawled out eating grapes in first class while the rest of us are packed like sardines in economy doesn't mean they're exempt from jet lag. The Four Seasons Hotel in Chicago knows how to beat it. When you have the wind knocked out of your sail in Chicago, this hotel offers a cure: a rejuvenation tea made out of anise, juniper, and fennel. Now if you're SOOO tired that you don't feel like going out to buy the ingredients, you can fax Thiemes Echte Thee in Holland for a 12-ounce bag (011-33-78-641-1686). The one thing that I adore about the Four Seasons chain is that they treat each guest as an individual. When a guest told a concierge that he had trouble sleeping because of the time change he found chocolate Z's written on his dessert plate! You can do this easily at home using a store-bought chocolate icing pen!

And if you're at this home away from home during a holiday, the hotel staff bends over backward to make the occasion festive. Easter baskets are delivered to every room on Easter Sunday. On Halloween, children are sent black witches' hats and pumpkins with candy, along with a toothbrush, toothpaste, and a reminder note to brush their teeth after they eat the candy! On New Year's Eve, chocolate horseshoes are given to guests for good luck! And kids can celebrate every day, when tub toys, milk and cookies, and personalized balloons are sent to their rooms. (I would love to be sent to my room!) Now, whenever I go to Price Club, I stock up on small kids' toys and tub toys. They're invaluable when it comes to making a little one feel at home in different surroundings.

Loews Hotels

All over the planet
800-23-LOEWS
www.loewshotels.com

"Don't fret if you forget!"

Whenever I pack in my dreams, I have a lady- (or man-) in-waiting, who knows exactly what outfits, accessories, and staples I need and packs them with perfect precision, never forgetting a thing. DREAM ON, LAURIN . . . The reality is I always forget a little somethin', but lo and behold, the brain trust at this worldwide company has come up with a great idea. Since female business travelers now make up 38 percent of the market share, Loews has come up with a "What Did You Forget?" closet that houses everything from pantyhose to pantyliners for the busy executive . . . and that's just the beginning! From a pair of cufflinks to replace the set that's sitting 1,000 miles away on your night table to a pair of socks, you can bet that you'll find a suitable substitute for whatever you "left behind" in this fabulous closet! No schlepping down to the gift shop required . . . it's pure convenience. In your own home, you may not be able to spare a closet but even a shoebox (stored under a bed) can house oft-forgotten essentials.

Rabbit Hill Inn

Lower Waterford, Vermont
802-748-5168
www.rabbithillinn.com

"The handwriting's on the wall"

Every once in a while, I'll receive a handwritten note from a celebrity, which I instantly treasure because of its personal panache. In our computer-generated society, a handwritten welcome note left on your bed typifies the perfect personal style shown at this 1795 former trader's tavern. I am also thrilled to report that penmanship is only the beginning! Heart and soul abound in every nook and cranny of this 21-room home away from home. Each room has a theme: for instance, "Victoria's Chamber" comes with its own subscription to *Victoria* magazine.

All the rooms have a diary for guests to share their thoughts. The thoughtfulness of the innkeepers is also quite unique. During turndown, your room is bathed in candlelight and soft music; a handcrafted heart-shaped pillow is given as a DO NOT DISTURB sign; other gifts include bunny-shaped maple candy, Rabbit Hill maple syrup, and a personalized box of Robert Frost poetry. When their beautiful garden is in bloom, you can expect to find rose petals sprinkled on your bed, along with a handwritten thank-you note on your last evening. It is generous of spirit for you to give parting gifts to your guests, and inexpensive little trinkets go a long way.

Charles Hotel

Cambridge, Massachusetts
617-864-1200
www.preferredhotels.com

"Cut the tension"

In case you arrive at your destination stressed by your three canceled flights, this hotel provides a gel that relieves tension on every nightstand. The management suggests that guests dab the gel on the sternum and solar plexus and breathe deeply for relaxation. Your local health food store should carry a variety of these gels, and Aveda also has an effective stress reduction cream in its line. Offer these products to your visitors and watch them melt.

Blantyre

Lenox, Massachusetts
413-637-3556
www.blantyre.com

"How to have a country picnic . . . Gwyneth style"

Gwyneth Paltrow spent many summers in Tanglewood, where her mother, **Blythe Danner**, performed. One of the Paltrow family favorites is Blantyre, and who could blame them? Set smack dab in the middle of 85 acres in the spectacular Berkshire countryside is this eight-room Gothic fantasy that replicates a grand Scottish manor, right down to the oatmeal served in Peter Rabbit pots. The rabbits never hop out the door, but what does go out the door here are five-course fantasy picnic baskets, decorated with flowers and ribbons.

During the Tanglewood music festival, the lucky guests unpack at their destination to find not only individual lidded boxes of food but also wine-glasses appropriate for their choice of wine, bottled water, candlesticks, table-cloths, a quilt for the lawn, and even **bug spray**! Who could blame a bug for wanting to land here? Sign me up!

When packing your picnic basket, follow the lead of Blantyre and add some unusual items. If candle-sticks are too fancy for you, try a citronella candle to keep mosquitoes away and romance close!

The Havana Riverwalk Inn

San Antonio, Texas
210-222-2008
www.slh.com/pages/s/sanhava.html

"A foolproof way to keep your house and wardrobe in order"

The ambience of this 33-room boutique hotel is like a scene from a Bogart and Bacall movie. Amenities are thoroughly modern with a hidden twist, such as individual thermostats concealed behind well-worn fedoras or cowboy hats! If you have an eyesore in your home that you would like to hide, try this hat method . . . and don't forget to add personalized baseball caps to the mix. Each room tells a unique story in accessories. A vintage photograph of three women dressed as angels sets "threes" as one room's theme. An antique clock is set at three o'clock. There are three stacks of pillows lined up on the bed, and other eye candy appears in "threes."

How does housekeeping keep all these themes in order? Each room is photographed in detail to ensure that each elaborate arrangement can be replicated daily. It's a great idea, but now that I know it, I hope I don't have to clean more often! And as long as we're saying cheese, I've always found it helpful to photograph accessorized outfits for those mornings when you have 53 seconds to get dressed. It helps to know whether that black and white checkered scarf you just grabbed will work with your suit!

Envoy Club

New York, New York
212-481-4600
www.envoyclub.com

"What to do when your home becomes the Heartbreak Hotel"

Sixty-three percent of all celebrity marriages end in divorce and, unfortunately, our national stats are not much better . . . maybe that's why the Envoy Club has such a high occupancy rate! I envy whoever was ingenious enough to come up with the "suddenly single program" at this NYC hotel. The Envoy

Club offers special amenities for recently divorced guests who've been sleeping on the couch for one too many nights. Self-help tapes, sound machines to combat long-term insomnia, referrals to local divorce attorneys, and aromatherapy candles are just part of this hotel's TLC. The concierge can even arrange a consultation with a psychic to get a head start on the future. So the next time one of your friends unfortunately checks into your heartbreak hotel (also known as your guest room!), you can offer more than a shoulder to cry on!

W

New York, New York
212-755-1200
www.whotels.com

"Dreamy sheets"

A favorite of the rock elite, this cool and groovy boutique/hotel offers every imaginable techno gizmo for the New Age traveler, but since everything old is new again, they also go back to the basics. In this busy metropolis, there is a working herb garden behind the front desk and planters in the rooms are full of live wheat grass instead of flowers. My favorite touch is the linen sheets strewn with mottos like "Sleep with Angels." I took some plain ol' white cotten sheets to my local tailor and had them embroidered with my favorite nighttime ditty! Sew charming!

Tides

South Beach, Florida
800-OUTPOST or 305-604-5000
www.islandoutpost.com/tides/

"The blackboard jungle!"

This hip hotel set in the epicenter of Madonna country cares about kids! Breakfast juice and Shirley Temples are always served in champagne glasses. Fresh edible flowers, such as pansies and nasturtium, are also included on breakfast plates. In addition to memo pads, Tides provides a chalkboard in each guest room. This novelty soon turns into a necessity. I couldn't give up the one that I now have installed in my own kitchen. Don't "erase" this idea—it's fun and functional!

The Little Nell

Aspen, Colorado
970-920-4600
www.littlenell.com

"It's a dog's life!"

Just up the road from **Goldie Hawn, Jack Nicholson,** and **Sally Field** is the Little Nell. Nestled at the base of picturesque Aspen Mountain, this cozy getaway has the distinction of being Aspen's only ski-in/ski-out luxury resort. Now, I realize it would be hard for you to re-create this ski-in/ski-out business, especially since your probably live in Tampa . . . but then again, hospitality should be re-created, especially hospitality toward animals! Pets are treated like royalty at the Nell. A welcome amenity (bone, toy, or bowl) awaits them in the beautifully appointed rooms. Your animal's name is written on a small blackboard, so that staff can greet their pet guests as they would their people guests. And, of course, the world-renowned chef is more than happy to accommodate special pet requests 24 hours a day. In my next life, I want to be a standard poodle who stays at the above-standard Little Nell. Even if there is no Rover or Tabby in your life, keep the name and number of a local veterinarian at hand in case some four-legged guests wind up on your pullout couch!

The Lodge at Vail

Vail, Colorado
800-331-LODG
www.lodgeatvail.com

"Cozy toesies!"

The creamiest hot chocolate or the hottest of toddies don't help your feet after a hard day of skiing. This luxurious lodge provides each guest, big and small, with a pair of soft, cozy booties. The comfort they provide is not just for infants anymore! Since slippers often slip off packing lists, always keep a spare pair for your houseguests! They are inexpensive and don't take up a lot of storage space.

Blackberry Farm

Wallard, Tennessee

423-984-8166

www.blackberryfarm.com

"Healthy southern comfort"

The philosophy of this estate in the Great Smoky Mountains is, "The answer is yes, now what's the question?" (kind of like *Jeopardy!*). Try this (at your own risk) with your guests and just hope they don't ask for the deed to your house! Some other less risky Blackberry Farm traditions include gold Hershey's Kisses piled in a bowl in each guest suite, heated bathroom floor tiles for invigorating mornings, and oranges studded with cloves and rolled in spices for natural aromatherapy. "Foothills cuisine" has become a quintessential part of the healthful Blackberry experience . . . no heavy southern comfort here, just wholesome and sumptuous southern hospitality. Chef John Fleer minimizes the saturated fat in some of his creations by using reduced wines or fruit juices in his recipes. Even if you are on a weight-gaining regimen (in which case, I'm jealous), be sure to have some low-fat substitutes in your cupboard when people come to your home. You don't have to cook separate meals, but you should offer simple alternatives, such as low-fat milk for coffee.

XV Beacon

Boston, Massachusetts
617-670-1500
www.877-xv-beacon.com

"Sample the luxury"

A stone's throw away from the setting of the TV hit *Cheers* is XV Beacon. Hidden among the highly appointed rooms at this Beaux Arts mansion are many high-tech goodies. Come to think of it, even my office is not that well equipped! I know it's not fair to ask you to transform your guest room into a high-tech haven, but their bathroom amenities can be yours for the sharing. Kiehl's peppermint foot cream, cucumber eye balm, jet-lag aromatherapy oil, and lemon verbena hand-milled soap are all yours for the price of admission. When stocking your own guest-arrival bin, go for the unusual! Many large chain drugstores have interesting sample-size products hidden in a corner for under a dollar! When I buy cosmetics in a department store, I always ask for some samples and save them for my guests. Even the fanciest lines have miniature selections—all you have to do is ask. Your guests may not get a color printer . . . but they will get color eye shadow!

Taggart House

Stockbridge, Massachusetts
413-298-4303
www.taggarthouse.com

"Share bears"

The philosophy guiding this 19th-century country manor is to ensure that each guest feels as if it is his or her second home. To accomplish this, Hinckley and Susan Waiatt, Taggart's proprietors, place a teddy bear on each bed that guests may cuddle during their stay. Herb sachets are put in the antique drawers to freshen up the old-wood aroma. And each bathroom has a heated towel rack. On a freezing winter day, a heated towel rack seems like such a luxury, but I got mine at Home Depot a few years ago for just $65.99. The electricity used to warm up the towel rack costs just pennies a day. It's more expensive for you to go to the drugstore and buy cold medicine!

Twin Farms

Barnard, Vermont
802-234-9999
www.twinfarms.com

"TLC is free!"

This stupendous New England inn once belonged to novelist Sinclair Lewis; now it belongs to anyone lucky enough to pass through its black iron gates! Anyone I've ever spoken to who has stayed at this magical inn has said that the experience is too hard to explain, because there are not enough superlatives to describe it! The meticulous thoughtfulness of the innkeepers, Shaun and Beverly Matthews, includes a welcome gift: a beautiful tray filled with port, sherry, and local cheddar, along with hand-warmers and Chapstick, in the winter; the summer tray may include fruit, homemade trail mix, maps, natural insect spray, and After Bite.

Room amenities include Origin products housed in a Vermont-crafted bath bucket. Turndown service can include anything from a cherry tart to aphrodisiac oil. The powers that be are always trying to improve upon perfection, but you don't really need a treat, since Andrew Harper's *Hideaway Report* voted these beds the most comfortable anywhere! I know it would be hard (and expensive) to re-create a Twin Farms experience, but the TLC that is always evident here is free.

The innkeepers have created their own "Referral List" on their Website, which cites other small properties around the world that exhibit similar TLC. Twin Farms is an inn for all seasons—they change their amenities to match the weather. That should be your clue to replace the sunscreen in your guest medicine cabinet with Chapstick during the winter, and substitute bug spray for cold medicine during the steamy summer.

Four Seasons Hotel

Beverly Hills, California
310-273-2222
www.fourseasons.com

"Many reasons to learn from the Four Seasons"

Superstars like **Elton John, Sharon Stone,** and **Mel Gibson** are sighted everywhere within these hallowed hallways, but even your Aunt Tilly would be treated like a star here. This garden oasis on the gold coast of Beverly Hills takes immaculate care of *each* and every guest. If this spectacular hotel were a cruise ship, it would be the "tightest" ship on the water. It's so well run by William MacKay, its general manager, that I'd like to nominate him for president (of the country, not just the hotel!). The Four Seasons keeps a detailed history of each client's stay, noting his or her needs and desires. They even knew that I liked the pool at 78 degrees (a fact that I didn't even remember about myself). Whether you open a computer file about your guests or jot a few notes in an old notebook, it's a great way to remember that your boss is allergic to your husband (I meant dog!).

Satin coat hangers, with padded shoulders for ladies garments, are provided for the guests. (Kmart sells a less luxurious version of these hangers that also work.) Hidden in the corner of the closet is an herbal potpourri bag that is not overpowering. I love its natural (nonoffensive) fresh scent. If you put potpourri in your guest room, take heed: make sure Uncle Charles's clothes don't smell like strawberry parfait when he leaves!

When you enter your room at this heavenly haven, the radio is always playing soft, soothing music. As a woman who frequently travels solo, I find this touch actually helps to erase some of the loneliness! And as long as we're talking music, when you pick up your car from valet parking, both your radio station and your seat have been left intact. No mysterious little paws have changed the channel for 48 seconds of their enjoyment! All of us should learn a lesson from that tip! And at the end of your stay (while you are wiping the tears from your eyes), they hand you a comment card that the management actually reads and cares passionately about. Spend a night in your own guest room every once in a while . . . so you can fill out your own comment card! My guest room is no Four Seasons, but not many are!

Chateau du Sureau

Oakhurst, California
209-683-6860
www.chateaudusureau.com

"The ultimate checkmate!"

Once upon a time (in 1991), a fairy-tale Mediterranean castle was built next door to Erna's Elderberry House . . . one of the most renowned restaurants in the land! This country manor house on Yosemite's southern doorstep seems as if it invented European hospitality. Yes, of course, they will whisk your suitcase into your opulent, outstanding room, but then . . . THEY WILL UNPACK IT FOR YOU and immediately steam any item that dares to be wrinkled. And speaking of unwrinkled . . . many Hollywood heavyweights have been drawn to the magic of Sureau! At the chateau, after dark, your nightclothes are laid out across fine Italian linens. At home, I love to do that with kidz pj's (and even stuff them with small pillows). Each impressive room here is named after an herb: The Mint Room, The Lavender Room, and so on. (I have a small antique blackboard, which enables me to change the name of my guest room depending on my guest!) In order to get into the rooms at Sureau, you need one of the heavy European room keys, which are attached to long silk tassels that are almost impossible to lose. I lose keys all the time, so I've started to attach scarves to the ends of my small American keys—and I haven't lost one since! On the grounds of this magnificent estate is a giant oversize outdoor chess set just waiting for a match! If you don't know how to play chess, you can definitely play "royalty," because every guest is treated like a blue blood! It would be difficult for you to re-create an oversize outdoor chess set, because you would need the pieces, but you could do it for checkers—with some chalk to set up the board and 12 black and red pillows or articles of clothing.

Hotel Bel-Air

Los Angeles, California
310-472-1211
www.bel-air.com

"Scent-sational scents"

The magic of this Tinseltown oasis is immediately evident, as guests cross over an arched bridge to enter a lush paradise. For over 50 years, this legendary hideaway has provided privacy and personal attention to celebs, industry big shots, and world travelers.

While all of your senses may go into overdrive at the Bel-Air, your nose will first alert you to the something special that is going on here! The avocado wood used in each of the 64 fireplaces on the premises perfumes the air with a crisp, fresh scent. If you're fortunate enough to have a hearth in your home, experiment with different types of wood . . . the fragrance can immediately change the atmosphere. Housekeepers at the Bel-Air keep linen requests on file . . . to bring out the satin, flannel, silk, or 300-thread count for their guests.

If your mother-in-law is sleeping in little Joey's room, lose the Donald Duck sheets and replace them with her favorites! One of my cherished "warm" touches at the Bel-Air can be felt while dining alfresco on the bougainvillea-draped terrace. The outdoor terra-cotta floor is heated so your footsies don't get a chill while you're dining! I always get chills at the Bel-Air—but never from the temperature . . . from the beauty. If you don't have the money or the inclination to heat your outdoor flooring, go back to basics. If you insist on staying outside when the weather beckons you to come in, have a wrap available for each person.

Furnace Creek Inn

Death Valley, California
760-786-2345
www.mammothweb.com/sieraweb/furnacecreek/

"Dandy dozing"

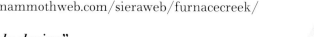

Legendary Hollywood folk such as **John Barrymore, Jimmy Stewart,** and **Bette Davis** would escape the rigors of being movie stars by escaping to the spring waters of Furnace Creek. The owners of this historic 66-room ranch have changed, but the charm hasn't: each night at turndown, a poem that celebrates the environment and the starry sky is placed on your pillow. Even if it's constantly overcast where you live, what a joyous way to enter dreamland! If poetry is not your thing, place a book of short stories by the bed: any reading that is manageable in one sitting is dandy dozing material.

The Golden Door

Escondido, California

760-744-5777

www.thegoldendoor.com

"Open the door to ultimate luxury!"

There are spas and then there's the exceptional one that lives in a class all by itself. Started 41 years ago by the visionary Deborah Szekely, this spiritual, sumptuous sanctuary constantly exceeds all expectations! You can do lots of stargazing here, but "The Door" believes that all guests are created equal. The beauty of the environment fills all of your senses. It's a retreat for your mind, soul, and body. It's impossible to take the incredible staff home with you, but you can leave with a piece of the miraculous chef. Michel Stroot's cookbook should be mandatory reading! Many of the magic potions sold by The Door can go directly from the refrigerator to the microwave. In the winter, I put my hand cream in the microwave for 20 seconds. Not only does it feel cozy, but it is actually more effective when heated. At The Door, when the sun goes down behind the mountains, it can get a tad chilly. No problem . . . a fluffy heated robe is yours for the asking. At home, I keep my robe over the heater, to provide warmth as I step out of the tub. Once a week, The Door offers a meditative silent hike. After a few awkward moments, it becomes an incredible experience to walk and not talk. I have made that silence a part of my strolls around the neighborhood. I so wish my neighborhood could be The Golden Door . . . it is in my dreams! The level of pampering at The Golden Door exceeds my wildest expectations, and it would be very difficult to re-create that feeling at home, but a little something is better than nothing. Whether you soak in a hot, steamy lavender bath or sip a hot, steamy cup of cocoa, allow yourself to relax and enjoy the moment! If you don't carve out time for *YOU*, no one else will.

Oak Knoll Inn

Napa Valley, California
707-255-2200
www.travelguides.com/inns/full/CA/3130.html

"XOXOXOXO"

With 600 pristine acres of vineyards as its background and guest suites that can only be found in dreams, it's no wonder that this Napa Valley gem has the reputation of being one of the best places to kiss in California. But I would like to kiss the feet of the innkeeper, Barbara Passino, who should be cloned! Her eye for detail is limitless, and her genuine warmth can light the fireplace (in your suite). Personalization is the Oak Knoll philosophy, and it can be found everywhere, from the made-to-order day-trip itineraries to the magazines and books you will find in your room. Customizing mags and books in your guest room is easy . . . and it may help you learn something about a topic that didn't interest you before your guest's arrival.

The amazing Barbara finds out your interests before you arrive and customizes your room. She even customizes your stomach! She keeps track of allergies and food preferences and jots down notes in a menu book (you can buy one at your local stationery store). She even writes down conversations during a meal! These notes trigger her memory even years later! I must admit that I now do this (thanks to Barbara), and it even helps in business! To establish a sense of place, this super gourmet chef serves local food in season. This is a nice touch for your own guests, especially when they come from far away.

Flowers are mandatory, but they don't need to be expensive. A $3 bunch of daisies in Grandma's chipped teapot is totally charming. As for teatime and coffee breaks: a French-press pot and tea leaves, not tea bags, are the rule at Oak Knoll. It takes the same amount of time to French-press coffee beans as it does to make instant! And Barbara's last little tip is a reminder that champagne should be served more than once a year. It's affordable now, often costing the same as a six-pack of imported beer! The only imperfection at Oak Knoll is that there are just four guest rooms . . . so only tell people you really like about this one!

The Peninsula Hotel

Beverly Hills, California
310-551-2888
www.peninsula.com

"Monogram mania"

Leave it to this house of sophistication to send surprise packages to some of their guests about six months after their stay. Having thoughtfully recorded whether the guest is a tea or coffee drinker, the hotel sends its special brew and exclusive cup and saucer to the client. You can modify this practice by jotting down the favorite things of the people in your life: when it's Aunt Tilly's birthday, you can then whip up a batch of the macadamia cookies that she was wild about at your son's graduation. The Peninsula also monograms its robes with your initials instead of its logo! Ask your local tailor to do monogramming for you. It makes a great gift, especially on unusual items such as pj's, underwear, or teddy bears.

Post Ranch Inn

Big Sur, California
800-527-2200
www.postranchinn.com

"Soap opera"

Barbra Streisand has sung in the shower here . . . who can blame her? I could move into the bathtub at this joint and be content for the rest of my life. Okay, you can't steal the tub, but even the soap at the Post Ranch Inn is an experience. It is specially made for the hotel, using flora from the local hillside. You can buy their sensational lavender or lemon verbena soap by calling 408-667-2200. But right now, sitting on the shelves of your local drugstore, are many more offerings than plain Ivory. For just a few pennies more a day it's time to upgrade your soap. Upon your departure from Post Ranch Inn, the management encloses a packet of wildflower seeds with your bill. It's a heck of a lot to pay for a packet of seeds—but a great thought! Seeds are a lovely little gift in a letter to a child or a grown-up child.

Sherman House

San Francisco, California
415-563-3600
www.slh.com/pages/m/manusac.html

"The name game"

Overlooking the Golden Gate Bridge is Sherman House, a mansion and carriage house that you'll want to make your home. When you arrive, you'll find stationery with your name on it on the desk in your room. This is a nice touch that you can re-create using your home computer!

Triple Creek Ranch

Darby, Montana
406-821-4600
www.triplecreekranch.com

"Dreamy beds"

Triple Creek Ranch is a unique, luxurious gourmet lodge nestled in God's country. Everything here is oversize . . . not just the peanut butter cookies delivered to your room daily. After a day of downhill skiing, you can go from your private hot tub to one of my fantasy beds of all time. These massive, magnificent, log-post comfort zones are so high off the ground that Triple Creek had to custom-design end tables and lamps to conform to their height. What a wonderful way to catch some z's! You feel as if you are sleeping in the clouds.

You can raise the bed in your guest room by putting a feather bed over the mattress (which should be mandatory) or by putting the bed on a platform. By the way . . . nobody steals the towels at Triple Creek. Instead, they ask for the design specs of the log cabins to re-create them for the future!

Inn at the Market

Seattle, Washington
800-446-4484
www.innatthemarket.com

"Herbal relaxation"

After a long day of harrowing travel, just walking into this French Country lobby, with breathtaking views of the Puget Sound, sweeps away any aggravation that the airlines might have caused! But just in case you still feel anxious, the management at this comfy boutique haven provides each guest with a travel pillow, filled with buckwheat hulls and fragrant lavender flowers, that conforms to his or her head, neck, and shoulder blades. And if you need more relaxation, reach for the eye pillow by your bed, which is wrapped in silk and filled with organic flaxseed and aromatic herbs. Don't forget to remove the eye pillow when you want to check out the incredible view from your window! You can buy travel pillows in most major chain stores. They not only work wonders on crowded airplanes but also make long car rides and living room couches more relaxing!

St. Regis Hotel

New York, New York
212-753-4500
www.sheraton.com

"Lights, laundry bag, action!"

The St. Regis Hotel, one of New York's great ones, has its own scented candles that give guests the familiar sweet smell of success when they enter their rooms. And a laundry bag and a lingerie bag await the items that may not smell so good, like their jogging socks. Your guests will appreciate any laundry receptacle—even a plastic garbage bag.

While the St. Regis does not go so far as to hang designer duds in its closets, you will be able to see what you brought! Lights in the closets are attached to motion detectors, so they go on and off when the doors are opened and closed. You can find these detectors in most hardware stores for under $75 and they are not *that* difficult to install. (Notice that I emphasized the word *that*.) The St. Regis is a classy joint with classy ideas.

Hotel Monaco

Seattle, Washington
800-715-6513
www.hotelmonaco.com

"Go fish"

You've left Fido at home, and you don't miss walking him. But you do miss having a pet. For a $15 fee, this hotel provides guests with goldfish. You don't have to walk them, but you are responsible for feeding.

Four Seasons Resort

Kailua-Kona, Hawaii
808-325-8000
www.fourseasons.com

"Splish-splash fun!"

During production hiatus in Hollywood, the guest list at this resort looks like the *TV Guide* listings! Plop me down in this Pacific paradise and the only amenity I would need is the ability to watch the water turn from cobalt to turquoise to azure! And when I turned blue in the face from not moving, I could always turn over and play connect-the-dots in the nighttime sky! But the management here offers everything under the Hawaiian sun, including some fun little touches for the little ones.

Kids are greeted with a very special Hawaiian welcome here. After all, a couple of orchids around a child's neck only provides limited fun . . . but a glass of frosty milk and fish-shaped cookies upon arrival help to make up for the long flight. And if fish-shaped cookies don't float your junior's boat, this resort offers a whole array of animal shapes—to shake, rattle, and roll. After a whole day of splish-splash fun, what kid wants to take a bath? The ones at Hualalai do. Each child's name is spelled out in colorful sponges, which are placed beside the tub. If you can't find alphabet sponges, you can always cut the kitchen variety to suit your needs. Can you spell F-A-N-T-A-S-T-I-C! (By the way, this also brings pleasure to grown-ups.)

Las Alamandas

San Patricio-Melaque, Mexico
328-555-00
www.las-alamandas.com

"The artful bedspread"

Picture this little piece o' paradise. Take 1,500 Garden of Eden acres . . . attach them to one mile of soft, sandy beaches . . . construct six extraordinary villas . . . stick chocolate-covered tequila bonbons and a frosty pitcher of cold lemonade in your maxi bar . . . and if this ain't Shangri-la, nothing is.

I barely have time to make my bed at home, but at Las Alamandas, bed making is an art. Each day, your name is designed on the spread with fresh flower petals. If fresh flower petals are beyond your reach at home, dried ones will do. You can buy them at reasonable prices in bulk at your local floral supply store. Since there are 80 employees for 22 lucky guests at Las Alamandas, each visitor has a dedicated waiter and butler/valet. The ratio in your home may not match this resort's, but you can still implement its ideas. Dinner in paradise can be served anywhere your heart desires . . . in bed or at water's edge. Your designated waiter has been known to set a full table (silver, candles, the works!) where the Pacific foam meets the shore, with a private Mexican músico trio serenading. It's hard to do this in Cleveland, but spread your wings during dinner. Every once in a while, choose to dine at unusual locales. You don't really need a designated waiter . . . all you really need is a designated imagination. Las Alamandas . . . my designated paradise hideaway.

The Lodge at Koele's

Lana'i, Hawaii
800-321-4666
www.lanai-resorts.com

"Aloha Paradise"

Seven miles off the coast of Maui is the secluded, exquisite island of Lana'i. It's no surprise that this pristine island resort has generated every travel award under the Hawaiian sun for its mouth-watering accommodations, superb service, stupendous sports opportunities, and divine gourmet delights! Now I know it may be hard for you to duplicate the natural beauty of this incredible paradise, but here are a couple of hints.

Although this hotel is relatively new, the owner, David Murdock, wanted the lush landscape to look as if it had been there for years. Whether you are landscaping a tiny window box or a grand backyard, mix some mature plantings with some new ones. That will give your greenery a tradition of its own.

To ensure that you are equally comfortable inside this Hawaiian paradise, the folks at the lodge have implemented a fabulous "nap-style" turndown of the covers on their ultra comfy beds. The beds are made in the morning, then the blankets are turned back. Individual duvets are placed at the foot of the bed, along with a note that informs guests that their bed has been prepped for naptime. This idea can be duplicated in your home. Simply place a light afghan or quilt at the foot of the bed in your guest room. Grab a can of macadamia nuts to ensure sweet dreams!

Las Ventanas al Paraiso

Cabos San Lucas, Mexico
888-525-0485
www.preferredhotels.com

"Star search"

At this resort, the stargazing is a little different from what I'm used to in my business. Each room has a telescope to help pass the time. Even if you live in a bustling metropolis, a telescope can keep kids busy for hours—and your neighbors guessing! And to cure "pet lag," Las Ventanas al Paraiso actually offers dual rubdowns for you *AND* your Rover. Who says it's a dog's life?

The Martinez

Cannes, France
011-33-04-929-87300
netlondon.hotelbook.com/static/welcome—06438.html

"Do the Cannes Cannes!"

During the annual Cannes Film Festival, the star-studded bustling lobby of this beautiful hotel is definitely the place to be! This Art Deco, grande dame mansion still captures the glamour and excitement of the Roaring Twenties with a very contemporary sensibility. Although this Riviera charmer contains 430 rooms, it is impeccably run like one big home by its general manager, Jean Louis Bottigliero. He treats his staff as family and every guest like a VIP . . . a philosophy we can all embrace.

At The Martinez, while you are doing your own thing in the magnificent *salle de bain* (that's French for bathroom!), the audio feed from your TV can be piped into the room. I know this doesn't thrill a lot of you, but this is an idea whose time has come for TV-aholics who don't have enough space in their bathrooms for a set. I can't tell you how many times my bathwater has overflowed during one last *60 Minutes* story, one last *Ally McBeal* romance, or one last *ER* cliffhanger! The engineer from The Martinez assured me that this project would take an electrician less than two hours to complete.

This colorful hotel also adds a splash of color to match its mood. During the film festival, the entire outdoor facade of this structure is bathed in different hues of lights! Try this fun and funky way to repaint your house with light (if only for a night!). And if you don't like the effect . . . just pull the plug—on the lights, not the marvelous Martinez.

St. Martin's Lane

London, England
011-44-171-300-5500

"Your personal light show!"

Ian Schrager, the ultrahip, ultracreative American hotel magician, has taken his cutting-edge lodging style across the pond for the first time. I wonder what "Her Majesty" would think of the transformation of this once-dull '60s office building into a kaleidoscope of color and light. Each of the 204 rooms has light-color dials that enable guests to bathe the white furniture in whatever tint suits their fancy. You can actually color-splash your room to match your mood! At your house, it may not be practical to install an entire light-color system, but just changing a couple of white bulbs or adding color gels can give your room a mini face-lift. And now that you've set the mood, you may want to keep the rest of the world out! At St. Martin's Lane, a string of silk daisies placed outside your door replaces the ol' DO NOT DISTURB sign. At home, you can implement this privacy policy by establishing your own solitary symbol for your bedroom or guest room door. Just make sure your kids take it seriously!

Hôtel de Crillon

Paris, France
011-33-144-71-1500
www.crillon.com

"Parisian perfection"

Whenever I stay at this historic royal palace, I feel like a princess . . . and that ain't bad. Managing my fairy tale is Phillipe Le Boef, who runs this palatial Parisian perfection. Flowers, chocolates, Taittinger champagne, and strawberries welcome you to heaven. Frequent guests sometimes receive a vase or a goblet carved with their initials. At home, you can re-create that unique amenity by buying and using a simple glass-etching kit. It's so easy! A personalized goblet would be a terrific and inexpensive surprise in your guest bathroom or on a nightstand. Because the City of Lights is so picture-perfect, this hotel offers special photo albums. Give your guests a throwaway camera to go with the album. The ultraromantic Parisian rendezvous offers poetry on your pillow and a special garment bag for that special dress—the one you don't want to spill red wine on!

At the hotel's world-class restaurant, Les Ambassadeurs, even your pocketbook is pampered. A footstool is provided to save your bag the indignity of being on the floor. And if the pommes frites (french fries) get cold—for shame! They are covered with a sterling silver bell to keep them warm. (I found that a soup bowl also works.) With all this beauty, history, and attention to details, who the heck even needs french fries!

Fiji

360-256-4347

www.turtlefiji.com

"Silence is golden"

Andrew Harper's *Hideaway Report* called this island paradise "as close to heaven on earth as you're likely to get." I wonder if that includes the 17-hour plane ride!

Those lucky enough to come to this private 500-acre island arrive by seaplane. At the dock they are met by a member of the fantasy-island staff, bearing fruit cocktails in flowered coconut shells—and so the pampering begins. I adore one tradition in particular. Every Saturday night on this heavenly island, dinner ends with a moment of silence, so that guests can take the time to reflect and count their blessings. Amen! This is a lovely gesture to add to meals in your own home—even if you live on dry land.

One Aldwych

London, England
011-44-01-71-300-1000
www.onealdwych.co.uk/

"Simple perfection"

The "Changing of the Guard" had a profound effect on me during my stay at this incredible hotel. I'm not talking about the guards at Buckingham Palace . . . but about the change within me. I've always believed that *more* is better: pack that vase with more roses; throw more pillows on that overstuffed couch. But after day two in this luxurious, contemporary environment, I began to see it their way . . . perfection through simplicity. I always found that notion to be cold, but it's certainly not at One Aldwych.

When you get to your room you find one absolutely perfect flower, a true work of art . . . and three pieces of incredibly beautiful fruit that Mother Nature must have worked overtime for, teaching you that less can be more. The owner of One Aldwych tested just about every moisturizer on the planet before he found the custom Parisian one good enough for his palace. His passion for perfection can be seen and felt everywhere on this property . . . from the Mozart playing underwater in the pool to the special water in the loo. I am now a believer in simple perfection. One Aldwych has shown me the way.

Le Toiny

St. Barthélemy, French West Indies
011-590-27-8888
www.letoiny.com

"Chairman of the board"

Superstars galore call Le Toiny their home away from home! Nestled into the hillside of St. Barts, are 12 luxurious plantation houses overlooking a turquoise lagoon fringed with coconut palms. Each cottage suite is filled to the brim with every amenity under the French West Indies sun! But it's not the Stair Master exercise equipment carried daily to each guest cottage or the bath goodies specially formulated by a pharmacist in France that guests cherish . . . it's the ironing board and iron hidden behind a teak and mahogany cabinet. Go figure: some of these guests probably haven't ironed anything for themselves in 20 years! I know that you most likely can't provide your guests with a Blue Lagoon (or **Brooke Shields**), but an iron is easily doable.

Hotel Cipriani

Venice, Italy
011-39-41-520-7744
www.orient-expresshotels.com

"Very Venice"

Princess Diana adored this hotel for its charm and its warmth, **Sophia Loren** for its pasta! Every large Italian family has a patriarch that sets the tone and tradition of its members; for Hotel Cipriani, it's Natale Rusconi, who runs this splendid landmark with perfection and precision. Most elegant hotels are not kid-friendly, but at the Cipriani, even small bathrobes are provided for babies when they go to the pool!

The sumptuous bathrooms are stocked with everything from hollyhock shampoo to vanilla talcum powder. Kitchenettes are stocked with different types of Cipriani pasta and sauces, so guests can cook for themselves. Odds are you don't have your own line of pasta and sauces, but it's nice to let your visitors cook once in a while. (Hopefully they'll clean up too!) Guests staying at the deluxe annexes of Cipriani clean up too: each is provided with a butler and a golf cart for mobility. Make sure that you provide some sort of transportation for your overnighters—even if it's just the phone number of a taxi service—so that your check-ins don't feel trapped. . . . But if I had to be trapped anywhere— *bongiorno* Cipriani!

The Merrion

Dublin, Ireland
353-16-03-0600
www.merrionhotel.com

"Back to basics"

If you possess the luck of the Irish, or any luck at all, you will one day stay at the marvelous Merrion. This five-star luxury hotel was created within four magnificent 18th-century terrace houses, but there's nothing old-fashioned about it: the Merrion offers each guest outstanding food, glorious gardens, and the latest technology. But at the end of the day, when every computer port is shut down, the Merrion goes back to basics. At turndown each night, a different poem by William Butler Yeats is left on the pillow, ensuring pleasant and thoughtful dreams.

Brenner's Park Hotel & Spa

Baden-Baden, Germany
011-49-7221-900-0
www.preferredhotels.com

"Menage-a-spa!"

This grand hotel can look back on over 125 years of glittering history, while still making history. In addition to its world-class 5,000-square-foot spa, Brenner's German ingenuity has come up with the first private "spa suite." It's a spa within a spa that offers a private place for parties of four to relax in. There is even a spa butler at guests' disposal. I am not suggesting that you and your in-laws hop in your bathtub together . . . it's just a reminder that you can turn practically any room in your home into a spa. An aromatherapy candle, bath gel, and soft music can melt the stress away. At Brenner's, your masseuse is not your **only** best friend. This hotel will also pamper your pooch! A dog basket is provided for your Rover, and at turndown, a doggy treat is waiting. It's a dog's life—and I'll take it!

Château de la Chèvre d'Or

Èze-Village, France
011-33-4-92-10-66-66
www.webstore.fr/chevredor

"Bonjour beauties"

I always behave because I'm hopin' that on the other side of the pearly gates
will be . . . Château de la Chèvre d'Or. This heavenly one-of-a-kind gem sits
1,200 feet above the Mediterranean, in a walled medieval village. The angelic
general manager of this cliffside wonder is Thierry Naidu, whose eyes shine
when he talks about this perfect property! It is important to keep up your love
affairs with the beauty and nature around you. Being blasé is so passé . . . I
only wish that you could steal this magnificent view over the Mediterranean.
Hidden within the lush gardens of lavender, lemon trees, and roses are tiny
speakers, each about 50 feet apart. With so many mini speakers sprinkled
around the property, music becomes a soundtrack to nature. Outdoor mini
speakers are affordable and not that hard to install, so you can match the
sounds to the scenery instead of blaring Sinatra from just a single audio
source. Hearing heavenly music when you least expect it is a gift. Château de
la Chèvre d'Or is music to my ears!

The Peninsula Hotel

Hong Kong
852-2366-6251
www.peninsula.com

"An extra set of hands"

A lot of business hotels provide single-line phones in the bathrooms. But at
The Peninsula, they've carved out space for a "hands-free" number . . . so you
can shave, bathe, order custom shirts, and save a business deal simultaneously.
You can order these phones from your local telephone company or private
vendors. They are also a mother's helper in the kitchen, where I can always
use an extra set of hands!

La Bastide de Moustiers

Provence, France
011-44-4-92-70-47-47
www.bastide-moustiers.i2m.fr/

"Chef's table"

Alain DuCasse is the only double four-star chef in the world with gastro-nomic temples in Paris and Monte Carlo. But his dream was to open a tiny, charming 12-room inn in Provence with an informal restaurant that serves food from the region. We arrived at the restaurant just as it was about to open and noticed that all of the loaves of homemade bread were simply sit-ting on the tablecloths without a bread plate or a basket.

After investigating this "plateless" situation, I learned that the chef's grandmother believed that bread should always sit right on a table to signify that every person deserves to live with-out hunger. She also believed that bread should not be sliced but pulled apart. And guess what? It doesn't cost a lot of "bread" to eat in this inn of perfection, a claim I can't make for DuCasse's other two fine establishments. Now, as far as I'm concerned, I have one less plate to wash!

At Hotel Why Bother? . . . Why Not!
It's always idea checkout time!